A Field Guide to Student Teaching in Music

Student teaching in the music classroom is a unique experience that incorporates issues beyond those encountered in general education classroom settings. Music educators plan for singing, movement, performances, rehearsals, score preparation, intensive parent involvement, budgets, uniforms, community outreach, and the list can and does go on. While general education texts may offer students advice on effective teaching strategies and classroom management, it is highly unlikely that these strategies will be fully applicable to the uniqueness of the music classroom.

A Field Guide to Student Teaching in Music is a practical guide focused on the link between music education coursework and the field-based aspects of the student teaching experience. It addresses general topics that are common to all music placements as well as those topics that are of specific interest to the general, choral, and instrumental music classrooms.

This text builds on theoretical materials typically covered in music methods courses, yet is not specific to any one particular teaching pedagogy, making it flexible enough for use in a variety of music teaching settings. It will guide students through the student teaching process as they make the transition from student to music educator.

Ann C. Clements is Associate Professor of Music Education at Pennsylvania State University.

Rita Klinger is Professor of Music at Cleveland State University.

D0166792

A Field Guide to Student Teaching in Music

ANN C. CLEMENTS
Pennsylvania State University

and

RITA KLINGER
Cleveland State University

Routledge
Taylor & Francis Group

NEW YORK AND LONDON

Please visit the companion website at
www.routledge.com/textbooks/9780415994583

First published 2010
by Routledge
270 Madison Avenue, New York, NY 10016

Simultaneously published in the UK
by Routledge
2 Park Square, Milton Park, Abingdon, Oxon OX14 4RN

Routledge is an imprint of the Taylor & Francis Group, an informa business

Typeset in Garamond and Helvetica Neue by Swales & Willis Ltd, Exeter, Devon
Printed and bound in the United States of America on acid-free paper by
Sheridan Books, Inc.

Library of Congress Cataloging-in-Publication Data
Clements, Ann Callistro.
A field guide to student teaching in music / Ann C. Clements and Rita Klinger.
    p. cm.
    Includes bibliographical references.
    1. School music—Instruction and study—United States. 2. Student teaching—United States.
    I. Klinger, Rita. II. Title.
    MT3.U5C54 2010
    780.71—dc22
    2009043145

ISBN 13: 978–0–415–99458–3 (pbk)
ISBN 13: 978–0–203–89047–9 (ebk)

Contents

List of Worksheets

Preface

A Field Guide to Student Teaching in Music is designed to guide the student teaching experience. The text is designed to promote thoughtful discussion by addressing the primary issues with which music student teachers often struggle. It is intended to "bridge the gap" between pre-service coursework and the practical experiences encountered during the music student teaching process. To encourage active involvement, this text is two-fold and consists of a textbook and accompanying online worksheets corresponding to each textbook chapter.

The primary purpose of *A Field Guide to Student Teaching in Music* is to provide music student teachers an opportunity to reflect on the student teaching experience and to gain insight into the multiple skills needed for successful, career-long teaching. Each chapter of this text focuses on a specific topic, and each topic stands alone, allowing specific issues and concepts to be discussed as they becomes relevant to the student teaching experience. Within each chapter there are several activities to encourage reflective thought and the sharing of experiences. Activities include the following:

- *Scenarios* – The scenarios provide examples of situations students may find themselves dealing with during their student teaching experience. The scenarios often provide typical, though somewhat perplexing, situations that will require student teachers to determine the best possible outcomes to remedy the presented problems.
- *Discussions* – The discussions consider particular questions and issues which may be addressed individually as students read the text, or may be a point of large group discussion in the student teaching seminar.
- *Cooperating Teacher Discussions* – These are issue-specific prompts that provide a starting point for initiating conversations between the student teacher and the cooperating teacher.

■   *Worksheets* – This text has multiple worksheets that are available online and available for download on the companion website at **www.routledge.com/textbooks/ 9780415994583**. The worksheets will guide observations, class discussion, and conversations between student and cooperating teacher, and provide activities relevant to student teaching. Worksheets are specific to topics within each of the chapters. Chapter 5: *Program Organization*, contains worksheets that pertain to the more over-arching duties, tasks, and responsibilities of music teaching.

To The Student

Congratulations on making it to your student teaching experience! As you are well aware, it is not an easy feat to have made it this far in preparation for becoming a music teacher. However, keep in mind that all of the coursework you have taken in music, education, and music education has well prepared you for the many challenges you will face in your student teaching experience. As you enter this new phase in your teaching career, keep in mind the coursework you have taken thus far and use those ideas, materials, and communications with faculty to guide your continued learning.

Student teaching in music settings can be a daunting task. Often this may be your first separation from the college or university setting in which you have spent years preparing. Along with this separation from coursework comes the separation from friends, faculty members, and possibly even physical location from the university. You may find yourself feeling alone in uncharted territory. The first thing you must realize is that you are not alone. You have been assigned a cooperating teacher or teachers to assist you daily and a university supervisor to guide you. These two allies are of paramount importance throughout your student teaching experience.

Along with the transition from the university setting, you are also making the transition from *student* to *teacher*. This transition takes time and practice. It is important for you to realize that from now on you will be viewed as a teaching intern—an adult, a leader, and a professional—in the school building and its surrounding community. While some of your university colleagues and peers may remain in 'student mode' for semesters, if not years, you will automatically be addressed by your last name upon the start of these experiences and have all the responsibilities that go along with this title. Regardless of how young you feel or how close in age you may be with your students, you are now the adult and from day one in your student teaching placement you need to begin acting like one.

With all these difficult transitions you may find yourself questioning what exactly you are doing in this situation. Please find comfort in knowing that every single teacher in this country has been through this experience! You are here for reasons, and those reasons are your love music, music teaching, and working with children and youth. As you delve deeper into the experience, you will have good days and bad days, and in the end the good days will outweigh the bad. This text will assist you in getting the most out of your student teaching experiences and ensure that you are as well-prepared as possible for a successful start to your career as a music educator!

To the University Supervisor or Instructor

This textbook is designed to be used as a companion to your university student teaching seminar or the course that student teachers take while completing their field experience. The Introduction serves as a reminder of the preliminary activities that will facilitate easing into a new student teaching placement. This section also aids in explaining the relationship between the student teacher, cooperating teacher, and university supervisor, while encouraging students to maintain open lines of communication with all involved in the process.

Although the chapters following the Introduction are logically ordered, individual chapters may be used in any order you find most relevant to your music student teachers' experiences. We realize that music student teachers within the same cohort may be simultaneously teaching in very different settings. Some may be teaching elementary general music while others are teaching high school band programs, yet all students typically meet together for a seminar or class meeting that corresponds to the music student teaching experience. The content of each chapter is specific to student teaching in music, but is also flexible enough to be applied to any level and area of music. Chapter 5, *Program Organization*, in particular, provides worksheets covering a breadth of topics that may prompt differing response from each student's experiences, and are broad enough to be reused for student teachers as they transition from one field placement to another.

It is our hope that the real-world scenarios, the discussion questions found within each chapter, and the on-line worksheets will motivate your music student teachers to reflect on their daily experiences at their student teaching sites, facilitate a positive relationship with their cooperating teachers, and stimulate lively class discussion.

Ann C. Clements & Rita Klinger, March 2010

Introduction

FIGURE I.1. Courtesy of Robert Thivierge.

This introduction will guide you as you begin making the transition from *music student* to *music teacher* and will focus on four main topics: 1) preparation for your first day and communication with your cooperating teacher(s); 2) understanding the relationships between your cooperating teacher(s) and the university supervisor; 3) adjusting to new environments; and 4) professional responsibilities.

Preparing for Your First Day and Communication with Your Cooperating Teacher

Most likely you have been assigned to a particular student teaching placement or placements based upon your needs as a student teacher. You may have received written or verbal communication about your placement previously, and may have had an opportunity to visit the school building. This section of the introduction will focus on introductions, developing relationships, scheduling, and becoming aware of basic school rules and protocols. If you have already experienced some of these issues, please continue reading for additional tips and advice for the next time they are encountered.

If you haven't made contact with your cooperating teacher yet, you need to do so now. Your university supervisor can connect you with them via a phone number or school email address. The first thing you will need to do is to introduce yourself. While your cooperating teacher will most likely have received information about you from your university, it is important that they begin to know you as a person and their future student teacher. Whether you choose to initiate conversation via telephone or email, it is imperative that you meet with your cooperating teacher face to face prior to your arrival, if possible. You may ask them to coffee on a weekend or after the school day, or invite them to dinner during the week. If you have recently moved into the community and are feeling overwhelmed, ask if you may visit them in their classroom at the end of a school day.

During this conversation, it is important to keep a balance of being professional and yourself. During your placement experience, you will be working very closely with your cooperating teacher(s) and you need to begin to foster a comfortable working relationship with them. In this relationship, you need to be able to ask for help, seek advice, and bounce ideas around. You will want to share your previous experiences and to allow them to share theirs as they pertain to this teaching environment. Keep in mind that your cooperating teacher will also have gone through a student teaching experience. It is a careful balance of speaking and listening. If you are feeling nervous, prepare a few questions for them to address. Some questions you may want to ask are listed below.

Questions to Ask Your Cooperating Teacher

1. What is your typical teaching schedule and how does this correspond with the overall school schedule?
2. When am I expected to arrive at school each morning and when does a typical day end?
3. Where do I park and how should I check in once I arrive at the school building?

4. What are my responsibilities beyond your classroom?
   a. Should I be prepared to assist with meal or bus duties?
   b. Are there important before school or after school meetings that I should participate in?
   c. Are there evening or weekend rehearsals, concerts or events during my time at this placement that I should schedule into my calendar?
5. What materials should I bring with me daily to assist in this experience?
6. How does lunch work? Should I be prepared to bring my own lunch daily or are there other options?
7. Is there a school dress code or dress expectations for faculty members?
8. Are there any particular rules on campus that I should know from the first day, such as no cell phones, no chewing gum, etc?

You may feel much more prepared, and possibly even relieved, after having an initial conversation with your cooperating teacher. Throughout student teaching, the less hesitant you are to ask questions, the more comfortable you will become. Be sure to ask if you may have a way to contact your cooperating teacher after school hours in case of emergency. Be sure to ask if they are comfortable receiving calls from you at home, and what kinds of calls they are willing to accept. Remember that if the issue should arise that you need to contact a cooperating teacher outside the school day, you must follow basic phone etiquette rules such as not calling after 8:00 pm unless it is an emergency and to be respectful of their need for a personal, non-school-related home environment.

Prior to your first day of student teaching, you should gather materials that will assist you with common tasks. These might include: paper and a writing utensil, money for lunch or a packed lunch, parking permit if one is required for your first day, any needed worksheets from this textbook, and a laptop computer (if desired). Be sure to dress professionally for your first day of student teaching, following the guidelines suggested by your cooperating teacher. The general rules are as follows:

1. Dress appropriately for the kinds of activities you expect to encounter.
2. Women, avoid revealing tops that will show your stomach or chest, and if you choose to wear a skirt, ensure it is longer than your fingertips. Be careful with overly high heels, especially if you anticipate movement or sitting on the floor with students.
3. Men, wear slacks (no jeans) and a button down or collared shirt. You may wish to wear a tie and/or jacket.

Cooperating Teachers and the University Supervisor

Throughout your student teaching, your cooperating teacher(s) and your university supervisor will be your main sources of information, communication, and feedback.

Your cooperating teacher(s) and your university supervisor have been selected for specific reasons. These reasons include their expertise in music teaching, their years of experience, their willingness to mentor a student teacher, and their belief that the student teacher process is important. Creating positive relationships with each of these people will make for a successful experience. It is extremely important that you realize, right from the start, that your cooperating teacher(s) and university supervisor are part of a larger team who are there to assist you through this process. Each member of this team has different, yet complementary roles to play.

The Cooperating Teacher(s)

A productive relationship with your cooperating teacher(s) puts you in a strong position to learn and become a successful teacher. In addition, it builds the foundations needed for a positive letter of recommendation at the completion of your experience. The relationship you build is dependent upon the way in which you view your overall experience. Are you truly prepared to learn from this relationship? Are you willing to adjust your teaching to fit this new environment? Are you able to trust the guidance of your cooperating teacher(s) based on their years of professional experience? It is important to keep in mind that your cooperating teacher(s) play two roles: they serve as both your employer and your instructor. This relationship begins with your very first contact, as described above.

It is important to refrain from making judgments about your cooperating teacher prior to knowing them in their unique school environment. It is not uncommon that before and after student teaching placements are announced, some of your classmates may make comments about the strengths or weaknesses of a particular teacher, music program, or school. If you hear such remarks about your placements, you are advised to ignore them or be cautious about accepting them as fact. You will make better strides at building a successful teaching team if you approach a placement with an open mind. It is truly impossible to judge a teacher or program unless you have in-depth, first-hand knowledge of the daily teaching environment.

It is likely that you will know little about your cooperating teacher(s) prior to your arrival at the placement. This may add to your general nervousness about how to begin building a positive relationship. One way to reduce your nervousness is to imagine that the roles are reversed.

- If you were a cooperating teacher preparing to meet your new student teacher, what would you want that encounter to look and feel like?
- What characteristics would you want your student teacher to possess?
- How would you like them to interact in your classroom?
- How would you like them to interact with you?

Most likely, the boss or employer part of you would be interested in someone who is professional, timely, dedicated, hardworking, and trustworthy. The instructor side may be looking for someone who is eager to learn, willing to take criticism, and dedicated to self-improvement. The answers to the questions listed above describe how you should act when you meet your new cooperating teacher(s).

It is likely that your relationship with your cooperating teacher(s) will go through various stages during the student teaching process. It is common that when you first begin a placement, you may spend a good amount of your time absorbing information quickly. During this stage, it is likely that you will be doing a lot of observation of your cooperating teacher(s) and their classroom routines. Through this stage you will become more comfortable with your surroundings and the daily procedures of the music classroom. You may also spend time assisting your cooperating teacher with tasks such as classroom preparation, becoming acquainted with students and learning their names, and adapting to the pace and atmosphere of the classroom and school building. You are encouraged to make the most of your presence by volunteering to assist with projects. It is a good idea to begin a student teaching journal at this time to document your progress and learning.

The second stage of your relationship with your cooperating teacher is becoming a teaching team. In this stage, you may begin doing some team teaching with your cooperating teacher(s). You may also be asked to contribute ideas to general lesson planning or be asked to select a few musical scores that you will work on with the ensemble. Sometimes during this second stage in your relationship, differences between you and your cooperating teacher(s) may become more apparent. They may teach differently from what you have experienced in your methods classes or they may have different philosophical ideas about teaching from you. While it may be easy to voice your concerns about these differences, it is important to keep in mind that no matter how different the cooperating teacher may be from what you currently view as ideal, they are the experts in this classroom. Additionally, you must keep in mind that there are lessons to be learned in all situations. You and your cooperating teacher have different experiences, different roles and responsibilities in the classroom, and different personalities. These differences should not stand in the way of learning.

As you gain more time in front of the classroom during this second stage, you may find that your cooperating teacher has feedback and criticism for you regarding your teaching. It is important to keep in mind that they are looking out for your best interests and the best interests of the students and their program. Unlike in most university classes, this feedback will be individual and somewhat personal, as it is directly related to what you are doing. Despite the feedback being personal, you must not take it personally. You must resist the temptation to become defensive. Avoid being judgmental or assuming that your way is right and the cooperating teacher is wrong. If you would like to discuss their comments, you must keep an open mind and ask questions that begin with "why," along with sharing your perspective. If there is a significant difference between your approach and theirs, you must follow their approach, after all you are a guest in their classroom and they will remain there long after your student teaching placement is over. The key to maintaining a positive relationship with your cooperating teacher(s) is to openly communicate about all issues. If you are feeling a breakdown in communication, speak to your university supervisor for specific ideas as to how to remedy the situation.

The third stage of your relationship with your cooperating teacher(s) begins when you take sole responsibility for a teaching segment. During this stage, you may be running a portion of or leading an entire lesson or rehearsal by yourself, using either your cooperating teacher's lesson plans or your own. Similar to stage two, this stage may include a large amount of criticism. The three main issues that can arise during this stage are: 1) receiving no feedback; 2) receiving what appears to be all negative feedback; or 3) receiving feedback while you are in front of the students. Each of these issues can be resolved by open communication with your cooperating teacher regarding what styles or forms of feedback or criticism work best with your personal learning style and fulfill the requirements at your university.

Scenario

Kate began the seventh grade choral rehearsal with the same routine that is typically included when they are led by her cooperating teacher Mrs. Wall. These included warm-ups of familiar descending patterns, ascending patterns, and a mixture of whole and half steps. Toward the end of warm-ups, Kate purposefully planned to include a warm-up pattern in minor, as the first song the choir was going to sing after warm-ups was in the minor mode. When she sang the first minor pattern, the students echoed back, but responded in major. She repeated the pattern and the students continued to struggle but got a little better. Her cooperating teacher, Mrs. Wall, who was sitting in the back of the class room, spoke out over the choir saying "The students don't know these patterns, have you ever heard us sing them before? Go on to something else." Some of the students repeated what Mrs. Wall had said and giggled aloud. Kate instantly became frustrated but did her best to finish the warm-ups and move on to the first song.

At the end of the lesson, Mrs. Wall reprimanded Kate again for straying from the typical warm-up routine. Kate simply listened to Mrs. Wall and accepted the feedback, even though she really wanted to explain her rationale for trying something new. For the rest of the day Kate was upset, but did not know how to approach the subject with her cooperating teacher.

Discussion

1. How would you have felt in Kate's position?
2. Did Kate do the correct thing in not voicing her rationale in front of the students?
3. Should Kate have voiced her frustrations to her cooperating teacher away from the students?
   a. If so, what would be the best way to approach this conversation?
   b. If not, what will be the effect on the student teacher–cooperating teacher relationship as the student teaching experience continues?

The University Supervisor

Your university supervisor has been selected to assist you in the student teaching process by representing the university setting from which you have come. Typically, such supervisors are familiar with your cooperating teacher(s), the school district in which you are working, general school policies and administration, and have years of teaching experience. They can be a good external sounding board for the experiences you are having within the programs to which you have been assigned. The university supervisor is your link to the university setting and also serves as a resource to your cooperating teacher(s).

Some universities employ graduate students to serve as supervisors, who have returned to the university setting after years of teaching. Other institutions employ retired teachers or current faculty members to serve as supervisors. Regardless of whom you have been assigned to as your university supervisor, they will have experience in the classroom and can serve as an important resource during your student teaching experiences and beyond, as you search for employment.

University supervisors often have diverse responsibilities and carry a very heavy teaching and observation load. Usual responsibilities of the university supervisor include:

- Scheduling and participating in observations of student teachers
- Writing reports on their observations
- Communicating with cooperating teachers regarding multiple elements of student teacher placement
- Maintaining relationships with the cooperating teachers, administrators, and other school personnel
- Keeping records of student teacher progress for state teaching certification offices
- Evaluating student teachers and assigning final letter grades, including providing references
- Staying aware of current job openings and communicating these with student teachers.

As university supervisors are often very busy people, it will be primarily your responsibility to foster a relationship with them. It is important to have a positive relationship with your supervisor as you are most likely to contact them when you are in need of immediate help or are preparing for them to observe your teaching. One of the best ways to develop a positive relationship is to first acknowledge that there should be a relationship. It is not unusual for your supervisor to be located some distance from your student teacher placement. As a result of this distance, they may not be fully aware of your daily or weekly experiences. One way to remedy this situation is to include them in your communications. You may even wish to send them copies of your daily or weekly journals, should you be writing about your experiences. A second way to build a strong relationship is to take a leadership role in the planning and scheduling of your observations. You are encouraged to contact them to arrange observations, as only you will know the best possible times and dates for observations in your placement. A final suggestion is to use their expertise. Do not be afraid to contact them regarding any difficulties you may be having in your placement. Often an outsider's perspective will give new insights into any situation. Additionally, you should not hesitate to contact your supervisor if you will be absent from your placement or if there is an emergency situation.

Adjusting to New Environments

Adjusting to the new environments of your student teaching placement can be stressful. The sources of this stress include separation from friends or family, departure from the university setting, adjustments to the pace of the school building, and the creation of new professional relationships. The key to adjusting well to new environments is findings ways in which to relieve these stresses and reduce anxiety. Some ways in which to do this are listed below.

- Maintain a positive self-image
- Ensure you are getting enough sleep and eating appropriate nutrition
- Schedule time outside of school to continue activities you enjoy doing such as socializing with friends, exercising, watching television or movies, or participating in music-making
- Do your best to prepare your lessons far in advance of your teaching
- Make to-do lists of all the activities you need to accomplish
- Plan ahead for larger events or projects
- Maintain strong communication with your cooperating teacher(s)
- If you are far away from friends and family, use electronic or other means to stay in touch
- Break up larger assignments into more manageable smaller chucks
- Do not procrastinate
- Try not to worry about things you can not change
- Keep an open mind and a sense of humor
- Set realistic expectations for yourself
- Allow yourself to place student teaching, and all that it requires, as your number one priority right now.

It is important to learn as much as you can in your new environment as quickly as possible. You primary source for information will be your cooperating teacher. While there may be multiple handbooks or guides that explain the rules and procedures of a particular environment, there are also numerous guidelines that are not stated clearly in a publication. This kind of insider knowledge is essential to understand the environment, and the sooner you know the environment, the more quickly you will become comfortable. Each school building's environment is different. Any teacher who has been in the same location for a period of time can identify these differences. Insider knowledge includes items such as knowing the various cliques or groupings among the teachers, what to say and what not to say in the faculty room, and how best to introduce yourself into that particular school's culture.

Professional Responsibilities

Many student teachers are surprised to find that the duties of a music teacher extend far beyond daily classes and rehearsals. As a teacher, you are accountable for the majority of these responsibilities. Often these responsibilities are either divided up between the teachers, allowing each to have specific tasks to fulfill, or they are rotated among the teachers, with selected teachers in charge of specific tasks on particular days. As a student teacher, you are responsible to take part in as many of these extra duties as possible. Your cooperating teacher can give you guidance on which activities would be most appropriate. Examples of these additional responsibilities include bus or meal duty, open houses and parent–teacher conferences, faculty meetings, and committee work. Many of the duties take place before and after school. While many outside of education believe the length of the teaching day is simply the hours that school is in session, all teachers realize that the hours in which students are on campus is only a portion of a teacher's schedule. Also, keep in mind that the school schedule denotes days in which students do not attend school, but frequently teachers do attend school for in-service workshops or other school-wide events.

As a music student teacher, you are likely to have many additional responsibilities beyond those of your non-music student teacher colleagues. For example, you may be in charge of leading school rehearsals, evening performances, weekend festivals, competitions, tours, school musicals, evening rehearsal, marching band camps, and the list goes on. Being a music teacher is a very time-consuming job and your student teaching experience is your opportunity to learn as much about these responsibilities as it is about daily in-class teaching. A good rule to follow is to arrive in the morning at the same time as your cooperating teacher and to stay each afternoon or evening until they depart the campus.

In addition to the responsibilities listed above, you must also recognize that you are still a college or university student and there will be assignments and class meetings related to your student teaching experiences. It is important that you communicate these responsibilities to your cooperating teacher. In addition to college or university responsibilities, you may also find it important to begin or maintain your relationship with professional music organizations. Most likely these responsibilities will impact on you with regards to student events, such as music festival and performances, and in professional development, conferences, and workshops.

one
Observation

FIGURE 1.1. Courtesy of Dr. Ed Brambley; www.flickr.com/edbrambley.

Observation is often the first encounter you will have with your new teaching environment. It is through observation that you will become familiar with the educational environment, a variety of instruction practices, management of classroom procedures, and the learning climate.

Classrooms are complex environments. Activities, materials, and lessons are in a constant flux dependent on teacher's preference and the students' needs and abilities. Even the ways in which teachers approach these materials and lessons change regularly due to an innate understanding of their students. It is because of these complexities that the student teaching experience is of significant value. Student teaching in a quality school music program may be the most significant part of your teacher preparation program.

In your methods classes and up until this point in your pre-service career, you learned and practiced observation techniques specifically designed to help you consider topics encountered in your methods classes. Your observations, though guiding you toward a career goal, were those of an outsider. Now you will begin to examine these issues as someone immersed in a school music culture.

Activities in this chapter invite you to address issues of self-development and personal growth opportunities as you make meaningful observations. This initial stage of teaching offers rich opportunities to observe, pose questions, and write about your learning process as an emerging music educator. Through your own filters of knowledge, attitude, beliefs, and values, you will process these experiences and reconstruct your own image of the teaching role. The teaching maturity gained during this experience may alter your beliefs and allow you to expand, accept, and understand differing ideas and concepts. In doing so, you build personal knowledge and come to know teaching at the level of practical everyday events.

Why Observe?

Getting ready for your student teaching internship can be a time filled with mixed emotions. Part of you will be excited to be going out into the schools to work with "real" children and youth, while another part of you may be concerned that you're not quite ready to meet the challenges you may encounter. These feelings are typical and to be expected. It may seem as though you have so many questions about teaching music in these new settings that you don't know where to begin. The most informative place to start is through observation.

Student teaching offers you an extended period of time to work in collaboration with an experienced on-site teacher. This experience is a partnership between the student teaching intern and the cooperating teacher. Each of you will bring your personal skills, knowledge, and beliefs or values into this teaching environment. The largest difference between you and the cooperating teacher is that he or she also brings in-depth knowledge of and experience in teaching. Through years of experience in working with children and youth, the cooperating teacher has been able to refine skills, increase knowledge, and periodically reshape their beliefs and values. Along with having mastered the practical knowledge of good teaching, the teacher also serves as a knowledgeable observer of the classroom environment. While experience alone does not make a teacher an "expert," it does provide important opportunities to grow professionally. Your cooperating teacher may have a different view of the classroom's musical environment than you do based on their years of experience. Through observation you will be able to better understand the who, what, where, why, and how of teaching and learning in this environment. Observation of the cooperating teacher will be the core of your initial experiences in this environment. It is the combination of these characteristics that will create a truly meaningful experience.

Meaningful Observation

Classrooms and schools are complex social, intellectual, and physical environments where the average teacher makes more than one thousand interactions a day each with different levels and nuances of meaning. In this multifaceted, fast-paced environment, it is all too easy to miss what you think you "see." As you immerse yourself in this culture and observe and record these experiences systematically, you will reflect on what you have seen, and you will gain greater insight into how and why teachers and students behave as they do.

- How does observing differ from 'watching' a class session?
- What should I be observing?
- How do I track my observations?

Two short scenarios are detailed below (Scenario 1.1 and 1.2). In each scenario, the student teaching intern has been assigned the task to observe their cooperating teacher. They have both gone about this in different ways. Please read the following scenarios and answer the questions listed below each scenario. These questions may lead nicely into a class or seminar discussion.

Scenario 1.1: Jason's Observations

Today is Jason's first day as a student teaching intern. As a dedicated trumpet player and conductor he asked to be placed in a high school band setting. His cooperating teacher, Ms. Smith, teaches three ninth-grade general music classes and two band ensembles. Jason has been asked by his college instructor to observe Ms. Smith's teaching during the first week of his placement.

Jason is eager to become familiar with his future students and the classroom setting. His first observation is a ninth-grade general music classroom. He takes out a pen and paper and begins taking notes on how Ms. Smith greets her students as they enter the classroom. Throughout the class period, Jason continues to take notes on Ms. Smith's interactions with the students and the activities that are done. Already Jason sees how he might do things differently from Ms. Smith when it is his turn to teach.

Ms. Smith's second period class is also a general music setting. Ten minutes into second period Jason grows weary of taking notes. On the surface, the structure of the lesson appears to be exactly the same as it was in first period. Jason becomes bored and starts doodling on his notes. He wonders how he is going to survive a whole week of observations in general music. He is eager to see the bands rehearse, as that is what he really wants to teach.

When third period begins, Jason is thankful it is the intermediate band ensemble. He again starts to take notes. As the students begin to warm-up, Jason realizes that the trumpets are slightly out of tune. He is surprised that Ms. Smith hasn't stopped the class to ensure that the trumpet section is in tune. As the band begins their first selection, he is shocked by what he hears: missed notes, imperfect rhythms, and poor breath support. Although Ms. Smith stops to address a few issues, she misses many errors and allows the students to keep playing. Jason makes several notes to himself about the lack of quality in this ensemble and how he will make adjustments and corrections when it is his turn to teach.

By the end of the day, Jason is tired of watching Ms. Smith teach. He already knows that general music is "not his thing." From his observations he feels all he has to do in general music is to create a lesson plan on a given topic and then re-do that lesson with each of the general music class. On the contrary, he has so many ideas that he would like to try with the ensembles, and he can't wait for his turn to be on the podium. Jason really feels he has a lot he can share with Ms. Smith about working with high school bands.

Discussion
After having read Scenario 1.1, discuss the following questions:

1. How does Jason feel about observing Ms. Smith?
2. What kinds of observations has Jason been making during the general music and band classes?
   a. How is he keeping track of the observations?
   b. Does he appear to have a good idea as to what to look for when observing?
3. What is Jason's opinion about Ms. Smith's teaching?
4. Do you believe Jason is making the most of his observation time? Please explain your answer.

Scenario 1.2: Sarah's Observations

Today is Sarah's first day as a student teaching intern. Through her experiences in methods courses, she has become most interested in working with young children in a general music setting. Her cooperating teacher, Mr. Jackson, teaches kindergarten through fifth-grade general music in one school building within his own music classroom. Mr. Jackson sees each of his classes once a week for 35 minutes. On a typical day, he will see nine individual classes from various grade levels. Sarah has been asked by her college instructor to observe Mr. Jackson's teaching during the first week of her placement.

Sarah is so excited for class to begin that she has her pen and paper ready to go before the students enter the classroom. The first-graders are lined up at the door and as soon as Mr. Jackson starts a CD on the stereo, they begin to march into the classroom. Sarah eagerly leans over Mr. Jackson's desk and writes down all of the information from the cover of the CD that's playing. She continues to take very thorough notes including small pictures of how the students are moving. She writes down everything that Mr. Jackson says and sings to the class. Working furiously to keep up, she realizes that she is on her third page of notes by the tenth minute of class. She continues to detail everything that is happening in the classroom including small transcriptions of the songs that have been sung. By the end of the first class session, Sarah's hand hurts from writing.

Sarah continues this furious pace for the remainder of the day. When the school day is complete, she sits down to review her notes. She has over 25 pages. Although she is well aware of the activities demonstrated in each class, she really doesn't know where to begin in analyzing what she has seen. She feels overwhelmed with the many tasks of teaching and begins questioning if this is really what she wants to do for a career.

Discussion

After having read Scenario 1.2, discuss the following questions:

1. How does Sarah feel about observing Mr. Jackson?
2. What kinds of observations has Sarah been making during the general music classes?
   a. How is she keeping track of the observations?
   b. Does she appear to have a good idea as to what to look for when observing?
3. What is Sarah's opinion about Mr. Jackson's teaching?
4. Do you believe Sarah is making the most of her observation time? Please explain your answer.

Both Jason and Sarah handled their observations differently. Jason focused primarily on the style of teaching done by his cooperating teacher. Sarah focused her observation on the classroom activities. Despite their different approaches, both observations were not as meaningful as they could have been. Both student teachers could have done a few things differently to dramatically change the outcome of their observations, which could impact the way they continue in their student teaching experiences.

FIGURE 1.2. Courtesy of Jason Bain/Sun Media.

Observation versus Inference

Observation is a scientific term that means to be or become aware of a phenomenon through careful and directed attention. To observe is to watch attentively with specific goals in mind. Inference is the act of deriving logical conclusions from premises known or assumed to be true. Inference is the act of reason upon an observation. A good observation will begin with pure observation devoid of inference. After an observation of the phenomenon being studied has been completed, it is appropriate to infer meaning to what has been observed. Adding inference after an observation completes the observation cycle—making it a *meaningful observation*.

One of the difficulties Jason encountered was a matter of observation versus inference. Jason did very little observing during his visit. Instead, he spent much of his time inferring meaning to what little he had observed. He didn't enter the observation with a clear idea as to what to watch for, and thus he became bored easily. Jason did very little actual observing. As a result, the inferences he made about Ms. Smith's teaching and the planned lessons were inaccurate. Had he paid more attention to what was actually occurring, he would have noticed the subtle differences Ms. Smith made with each general music class and would have had a better understanding of her decision-making during the band rehearsal.

Sarah, on the other hand, did a tremendous amount of observing with very little inference of meaning. While Sarah meticulously wrote down every event and every detail of Mr. Jackson's teaching, she did not infer levels of importance to what she was watching. No single teaching episode or student reaction registered as more interesting or important than another. At the end of her day, she was overwhelmed with observation notes and unable to infer deeper meanings to all she had seen.

Worksheet 1.1 highlights the differences between observation and inference. Aim to complete worksheet 1.1 independently and be able to discuss your results in your seminar or class.

Worksheet 1.1

Observation versus Inference

Observe the images below and describe in narrative form what is happening in each situation.

Description:

Description:

Description:

Description:

Group Discussion

In small groups, or as a class, discuss your observations. Remembering the differences between observation and inference, as described in the chapter, check your work and the work of others to determine if the observations included any forms of inference.

Did you or others:

- Make assumptions about the individuals or activities?
- Include reflective statements about individuals or activities?
- Include statements that could be perceived as personal biases?

1. What is the role of pure observation?
2. What is the role of making inferences?

Guidelines of Observation

There are no set rules for how to conduct an observation. There is, however, a systematic approach to observing. The following are a set of guidelines to assist in the systematic observation of music classrooms.

- Guideline 1: *Each observation should have a specific well-defined purpose.* This requires that you identify a phenomenon of interest. In a typical music class session, there are a multitude of phenomena that can be observed. Having a firm idea of what you want to examine before the class starts is the only way to create a meaningful observation.
- Guideline 2: *Write or journal only pure observations.* You should begin by only "presenting the facts." Although it is very tempting to search for deeper meanings right from the start, it is imperative to know exactly what is going on first. This means that you must hold off on your questioning or hypothesizing of why an event happened until the teaching cycle is completed. Jason struggled with this during his observation. He chose not to simply present the events and occurrences but instead to focus on possible meanings for those events he did observe.
- Guideline 3: *Determine the relevance of what is being observed.* It is common for student teachers to write down all that they see in the attempt to be through; however, it is impossible to see everything that is going on in a class session. Sarah gave in to this temptation and wound up with so many notes that she didn't know how to make sense of any of them. It is best to start with a particular phenomenon in mind and then screen each occurrence of this phenomenon for significance. In order to determine what is important at the moment, you must use self-reflection. Is the occurrence interesting to you? Does it leave you with questions as to why or how it occurred? Has it left an impact on you worthy of further investigation or later discussion with your cooperating teacher? If so, these are the events or incidents on which you will want to focus your observations.
- Guideline 4: *Turn observations into inferences.* The purpose of an observation is to draw meaning from events witnessed in the classroom. Part of this process requires you to question what occurred and to make logical assumptions as to why or how events transpired. After you have carefully noted events of significance, it is important to make thoughtful assumptions as to why these events occurred. At times you will be tempted to make inferences while you are observing. Avoid this temptation! It is always a good idea to reflect back on the phenomenon after the class session has ended and you have allowed yourself some time to think through the events. Remember that inference is a form of speculation, and it is important to use terms in your writing such as "It appears that the learner," "It's my belief," "In my estimation," and so forth. This attention to language shows that you are focused mainly on the observed and prevents you or others from labeling without solid justification. Jason needed to observe more and make fewer inferences. When he did use inferences, he should have used terms such as those listed above, which allow for the expression of his personal assumptions.

Discussion

The guidelines listed above come from common practices in qualitative social science research. One of the primary fields in social science research is anthropology, which is the scientific study of the origin, behavior, physical, social, and cultural development of humans. Anthropologists spend a great deal of time living within the cultures and among the people who interest them.

Pretending that you are an anthropologist studying the culture of the student teaching seminar or class, discuss the environment as it pertains to each of the guidelines listed above.

Observation Perspective

It is important to recognize and understand your perspective when observing. Most student teaching interns are coming directly out of a college or university community, which can influence their observation and inference techniques in both positive and negative ways. It is, of course, a positive in that many of the lessons and techniques from music and education methods classes that have prepared you to enter the teaching field are still close at hand in your recent memory. Because of that, however, there is a natural tendency to view the observation from a theoretical rather than practical perspective because you lack the insider knowledge that can only be gained with teaching experience. In addition, you are just beginning to understand the climate and structure of your particular student teaching setting. In short, your experiences as a student are likely to influence the ways in which you observe the classes and view your cooperating teacher. It is important to partially erase your conditioning as a student and to begin to see yourself as an "emerging insider." This will allow you to view the music program, your cooperating teacher, and your student teaching environment with a fresh set of eyes.

Worksheet 1.2 is a good way in which to familiarize you with the classroom environment. Use this worksheet during your first visit with your cooperating teacher to document the set up of the instructional environment from the teacher perspective.

Worksheet 1.2
Observing the Instructional Environment

Name: _____

Subject/Grade Level Observed:_____

Observation Date: _____

As you begin to observe, it is important to have a good understanding of the location(s) in which you will be teaching. Remember that you are a guest in this environment and should not be critical of the classroom setting. Instead, focus your attention on the "where and why" of the environment.

Draw a map of the music classroom environment that indicates the following items. If you are teaching in various non-music specific locations, draw several smaller maps that indicate the space available for music activities. Then respond to the points below.

■   Arrangement of desks, tables, chairs, risers, etc.
■   Teacher work area or office
■   Student storage areas and/or classroom instrument storage or lockers
■   Learning centers/stations
■   Resource materials such as bookshelves, drawers, etc.
■   Equipment such as drinking fountain, sink, pencil sharpeners, bathroom, telephone, computers, etc.
■   Bulletin and chalk/white boards
■   Anything else you think is important in the environment.

1. How does the set up of this classroom(s) contribute to student learning?

2. Is it possible or feasible to rearrange the classroom environment for various activities? If so, how can this be done?

3. How far away for the music-teaching environment are the following locations?

    a. School office:
    b. Custodian's office:
    c. Drinking fountains:
    d. Bathrooms:
    e. Lunchroom/cafeteria:
    f. Performance areas:
    g. Playground, practice fields, practice rooms, or instrument storage:

4. If appropriate and available, ask your cooperating teacher for seating charts that indicate student names and attach a copy to this worksheet to help you learn names.

5. What do the contents and the layout of this classroom(s) say about the music activities valued by the cooperating teacher or school building?

Cooperating Teacher Discussion

Have a discussion with your cooperating teacher regarding the room set up. Include questions about where to find specific kinds of materials, such as textbooks, resources, the music library, and instruments and instrument repair supplies. Ask why the room is organized as it is and how this organization facilitates student learning.

Approaches to Observation

Observation is the primary means through which you can gain information about your new teaching environment. There are various approaches to conducting observations that may guide your practice in the field. These approaches include a log-based format, in which you observe and note specific behaviors at specific times, and a narrative format, in which you write descriptive narratives about what you are observing (typically this is done through journaling). Once you have completed an observation, you must turn your attention to inferring meaning to what you have witnessed. This process is commonly accomplished through reflective questioning.

In addition to selecting the format in which the observation will be recorded (log or narrative), it is important to know what you wish to observe. Prior to starting each observation you must have a clear picture in mind of what you are looking to observe. Since music teaching is a complex phenomenon, there are many aspects of the classroom environment worthy of observation. Some of these aspects include: 1) instructional practices; 2) differentiated instruction; 3) classroom management; and 4) learning climate. While this list does not contain every element worthy of observation, it will serve as our starting point for inquiry and discussion.

Many teacher-education programs require that you keep a log or narrative journal of your observations during student teaching. Some programs require a specific kind of observation form while others allow a more open-ended approach. In either case, your observations are intended to serve as a means for describing the events you witness and to reflect on those events in order to infer meanings. Through this process you will be giving thought to what you observe and how it impacts on you. Over time you will see changes in the quality of your observations and in your line of questioning and thinking about particular incidents. When you complete your field experiences, you will have chronicled your experiences and your logs and journals will serve as a map to your personal and professional growth.

Log-Style Observations

A log observation uses a standardized form to analyze when particular events happen. It is intended to serve as a record of both the class period and significant occurrences that attract your attention. This form allows you to follow the natural flow of the classroom and the lesson. The log form asks you to document the time an event occurred and to describe the event. After watching a complete teaching episode, you are asked to reflect on a significant event. You should reflect on incidents and activities that make an impact on your thinking, such as moments that impress you, are educationally important, disturb you, or challenge or confirm your thoughts on teaching. Worksheet 1.3 is a sample log observation form. This form can be duplicated and used for multiple settings and class meetings.

Worksheet 1.3
Observation Log Format

Name: _____

Subject/Grade Level Observed: _____

Observation Date: _____

A log-based format is intended to help you document and reflect on your observation. You should describe incidents observed and activities as objectively as possible. You may choose to write down any events that make an impact on your thinking, such as moments that impress you, are educationally important, disturbed you, or challenge or confirm your thoughts on teaching. These events, whether positive or negative, should be selected and described because they are critical incidents of learning. This worksheet may be photocopied and used multiple times.

Please keep in mind the difference between observation and inference. This log should include observations only. Inferences can be described at the conclusion of the worksheet.

Time   Incidents /Activities

_____   _____

_____   _____

_____   _____

_____   _____

_____   _____

_____   _____

_____   _____

_____   _____

_____   _____

_____   _____

_____   _____

_____   _____

Significant event(s):_____

Description:

Analysis:

> **Cooperating Teacher Discussion**
> Have a discussion with your cooperating teacher regarding events you
> found to be significant. If you're having trouble analyzing these events,
> ask for assistance as to why these events happened and what they mean.

Narrative-Style Observations

A narrative observation is similar to journaling in that there is no set format. Narrative observations allow the observer to write freely about the events and occurrences observed. A positive attribute about this form of observation is that the observer can detail events to a greater degree than in the log observation. A drawback is that the observer can often lose sight of significant events and begin to simply write every element of the classroom environment. You are encouraged to experiment with narrative observations in a notebook or journal. Be sure to write pure observations during the class segment and return later to reflect inferences on the situations observed.

Worksheet 1.4
Observation Narrative Format

Name: _____

Subject/Grade Level Observed:_____

Observation Date: _____

A narrative format is intended to help you document and reflect on your observation. You should describe incidents observed and activities as objectively as possible. You may choose to write down any events that make an impact on your thinking, such as moments that impressed you, seem educationally important, disturbed you, challenged or confirmed your thoughts on teaching. These events, whether positive or negative, should be selected and described because they are critical incidents of learning. This worksheet may be photocopied and used multiple times.

_____
_____
_____
_____
_____
_____
_____
_____
_____
_____
_____
_____

Significant event(s): _____
Analysis:

Cooperating Teacher Discussion
Have a discussion with your cooperating teacher regarding events you found to be significant. If you're having trouble analyzing these events, ask for assistance as to why these events happened and what they mean.

1) Instructional Practices

A possible focus for an observation may be to document the instructional strategies employed by your cooperating teacher. Teachers must manage the learning environment to enable students to achieve the objectives established in the lesson. Issues of instructional practice include the ways in which class is formally started, how the teacher determines students' prior knowledge, the use of visual organizers, small and individual group instruction, and the teacher's awareness of student understanding. Worksheet 1.5 may help guide your observation and reflection on the instructional process in order to acquire a more comprehensive understanding of the teaching process.

Worksheet 1.5
Observing Instructional Practices

Name: _____

Subject/Grade Level Observed:_____

Observation Date: _____

Teachers must manage the learning environment to enable students to achieve the objectives established for the lesson. This observation form may help guide your observation and reflection on this instructional process in order to acquire a more comprehensive understanding of the teaching process.

Answer the following questions while observing your cooperating teacher. You are strongly encouraged to reflect back on your answers at the conclusion of the lesson to add in more detail and reflection.

1. How does the teacher focus the attention of students at the beginning of the class? If this is an elementary setting, how do students enter and exit the room?

2. How does the teacher determine the students' prior knowledge of a subject or concept?

3. Does the teacher use a visual organizer or post an instructional outline to help direct student learning? When and how is it used?

4. If the students are assigned independent or small group work, what does the teacher do to ensure students understand the instructions? Is there more than one strategy for providing instruction?

5. If students are assigned cooperative learning groups, when and how does the teacher give the instructions for the group work? How are the groups selected?

6. How does the teacher assess student understanding?

7. What instructional strategies encourage participation of all students during large and small group work?

8. Does the teacher provide additional instruction while the students are working/playing? If so, how is this done?

Cooperating Teacher Discussion
Review this worksheet with your cooperating teacher and discuss the various issues you have observed. For each question listed above, ask your cooperating teacher if what you observed is typical on a daily bases. Ask for suggestions and guidance on how you can maintain similar techniques when you begin to teach.

2) Differentiated Instruction

The way in which information is provided to students changes by course, grade level, and even by class period. A good teacher will adapt teachings to meet the needs and abilities of their students. This variety in instruction is purposeful and worthy of observation. Detailed observation of multiple class settings will reveal both dramatic and slight differences. Worksheet 1.6 will guide you in determining these differences and drawing inferences as to why these differences have occurred.

Worksheet 1.6
Observing Differentiated Instruction

Name: _____

Subject/Grade Levels Observed: _____

Observation Dates: _____

Activities and the ways in which information is provided to the students often vary between classes or grades. This is particularly true for teachers who instruct more than one ability or grade level. It may also be true for teachers who have multiple sections of the same grade level.

For this assignment you will need to observe your cooperating teacher working with two different classes. These classes may be the same or different ability or grade levels, but *should be* the same content emphasis. Observing classes with two different content emphases, such as a band class and a choir class, will make comparisons more difficult.

Example observations:
- An intermediate and an advanced band rehearsal
- A first and a third grade general music class
- Two different seventh-grade general music classes.

You are asked to take narrative observations on events in each class or use a photocopy of the Log Observation Format (Worksheet 1.3) for each class. After completing these observations, answer the following questions.

1. How does the teacher introduce the class topic or focus for the day to attract students' attention on the lesson to be taught in each class setting?
    Class 1:

    Class 2:

2. List and briefly describe the different instructional techniques that were used during the lesson by class.
    Class 1:

Class 2:

3. If there were instructional differences by class, why do you believe these differences occurred? How did these instructional differences affect student learning?

4. Did you notice any differences in the mannerisms or teaching style of your cooperating teacher between these two different groups of students? Please explain why you believe there was or was not a difference.

5. Were there any differences in the pacing or time it took to teach elements of the lesson based on class? Please explain why you believe there was or was not a difference.

Cooperating Teacher Discussion
Please review this worksheet with your cooperating teacher and discuss the various issues you have observed. If there were differences in instruction between the classes discuss the difference you observed and ask for reflection from your cooperating teacher.

3) Classroom Management

It is important to understand the ways in which student behavior guidelines are expressed and managed in a music classroom setting. Each school building will typically have its own discipline code. This code is utilized by the classroom teacher alongside his or her own policies and procedures. Music teachers often establish proactive management systems as well as reactive disciplinary measures to prevent and deal with behavioral issues in the music classroom. Observing behavioral expectations and the management of student behavior during a lesson is an important exercise. Worksheet 1.7 will assist you in communicating with your cooperating teacher about management issues and then observing these practices in action.

Worksheet 1.7
Observation of Classroom Management

Name: _____

Subject/Grade Level Observed:_____

Observation Date: _____

Managing a classroom full of students is a daunting task. In order to familiarize yourself with the procedures and policies of classroom management used in your placement(s), it is important to discuss issues related to management with your cooperating teacher and observe these ideas in context.

Cooperating Teacher Discussion
Discuss the following issues of classroom management with your cooperating teacher:

- Establishing a positive learning environment
- Issues of transition from one activity to another
- The use of positive/negative reinforcements
- Consequences for inappropriate behavior
- Verbal classroom control techniques
- Non-verbal classroom control techniques
- Overall classroom policies for behavior
- School-wide policies for student behavior
- Strategies for managing students who consistently display inappropriate behavior
- What should be done in emergency situations, such as fights, out of control behavior, extreme bullying, etc.

After a discussion with your cooperating teacher regarding classroom management, observe a class and answer the following questions:

1. How does the teacher establish behavior expectations at the beginning of the class period?

2. How does the teacher establish a positive instructional learning environment?

3. What details does the teacher manage at the beginning of a class period or when implementing class transitions?

4. What positive/negative reinforcements are used during class?

5. Do students appear to understand the consequences for inappropriate behavior?

6. What verbal classroom control techniques does the teacher use?

7. What non-verbal classroom control techniques does the teacher use?

8. How are the classroom rules defined and adhered to during large and small group activities?

9. How does the teacher bring closure to the class period?

4) Learning Climate

The learning environment of a classroom is a large determinate in the extent to which students feel comfortable and enjoy being in a given class. Elements that affect the learning environment include the routines used, the attitudes of students and the teacher, the student comfort in asking questions, teacher expectations for participation, and the use of praise and reprimand. Worksheet 1.8 focuses an observation of elements that can affect students' desire to be engaged and learn.

Worksheet 1.8
Observing Learning Climate

Name: _____

Subject/Grade Level Observed:_____

Observation Date: _____

The ways in which students feel about the classroom coupled with the techniques teachers use for monitoring activities contribute greatly to the classroom learning climate.

   After completing several observations of your cooperating teacher, answer the following questions about learning climate. This reflective activity may lean more toward inference than pure observation.

1. How do students enter the room?

    a. Are they energetic, enthusiastic, lethargic?
    b. How do you think they feel about coming to this class?

2. Do they know the routine for entering the classroom, such as finding their seats, getting out instruments or music/texts?

3. What kinds of attitudes do you observe? Are they respectful of one another and the teacher?

4. Do students appear to feel comfortable asking questions during class time? Explain your answer.

5. How do the answers to questions 1–4 influence the climate of the room?

6. Are teacher expectations for student behavior, participation, and progress obvious to all? If so, how are they communicated?

7. Are students accountable for their own behavior and learning? If so, how is this demonstrated?

8. Is assessment teacher or student driven, or is it a combination of both?

9. Does the teacher "praise" the students and their work? If so, how?

10. Describe the pace of the lesson. Fast, moderate, or slow?

11. How do the answers to questions 6–10 influence the climate of the room?

Reflecting on Your Observations

Now that you have completed your entrance into the field as an emerging professional, it is important for you to reflect on your observations to begin to infer meaning and draw conclusions about your particular teaching and learning environment. Knowing that the meaning you infer from your observations is context-dependent and may be based on more than meets the eye, you will want to seek out additional sources of information both inside and outside the music classroom to draw your conclusions.

Many of your worksheets have asked that you dialogue with your cooperating teacher to learn more about the phenomenon that you have observed. Throughout the student teaching process your cooperating teacher will be an invaluable resource for assisting you in creating inference and building meaning from what you are observing. In addition to your cooperating teacher, there are many other sources to assist you in building meaning: talking with and observing students outside the music classroom, in other school settings and at play; communicating with other school faculty and administrators; and examining materials such as music and school-wide handbooks, school-wide disciplinary policies, school, district, or state-wide academic guidelines, and local, state, and national policies and laws are all sources of information to help place your observations in context. Your cooperating teacher and/or university supervisor can assist you in finding these kinds of materials.

Worksheet 1.9
Inferring Meaning from Your Observations

Name: _____

Subject/Grade Level: _____

Date: _____

Select a single observation from worksheets 1.5–1.8. Complete the task below. Base your response on the worksheet you selected.

Observation worksheet selected for this assignment: _____

Choose one phenomenon or area of interest that you witnessed during that observation that you would need to know more about in order to more fully understand. It can be an event in the lesson or rehearsal that occurred, an interaction between teacher and student or students and student, or it can be related to classroom policy or procedure.

Briefly describe your selected area of interest:

_____

_____

_____

_____

Using as many available resources as possible, begin an investigation of that phenomenon. Write a two-page summary of your investigation indicating how the additional sources enhanced your understanding of the event. The following checklist can help guide your thinking as to what sources may be available.

Indicate which of the following materials/sources you have used to complete this investigation.

Music Ensemble or Classroom Handbooks	District Policy Publications	State Standards, Learning Outcomes or Objectives	Education Periodicals or Journals
School-wide Handbooks	State or National Policy Publications	National Standards, Learning Outcomes or Objectives	Materials or Texts from Previous Coursework
District Wide Handbooks	Music Library or Student Textbook Sources	Parents or Booster Clubs Materials/ Community Sources	The Internet
School-wide Policy Publications	Local (School or District) Learning Outcomes or Objectives	Music Education Periodicals or Journals	Other: _____

Indicate which of the following conversational or additional observational sources you have used.

Dialogue with Cooperating Teacher	Dialogue with Staff (non-faculty)	Observation of Students Socializing	Observation of Administrative Practices
Dialogue with non-Music Teacher	Dialogue with University Supervisor	Observation of Students at Play	Observation of Rehearsal Outside of School Day
Dialogue with Students	Dialogue with Parent(s)	Observation of Students elsewhere at School Site	Observation of Concert or Performance
Dialogue with Administrator	Dialogue with Community Members	Observation of non-Music Teachers	Other: _____

See website

Your student teacher experience is an exciting stage in your personal and professional development. It bridges the gap between previous experiences as a music education student and your future as a music educator. To make the most of your initial experiences in your new student teaching environment, you need to observe diligently and reflect thoughtfully on your observations in order to infer meaning. Through the selection of events or incidents that intrigue and challenge you, and by seeking out how and why these events occurred, you will begin to build the repertoire of skills needed for continued success during your student teaching experience. During this process it is important to allow yourself to reflect on your personal attributes and skills, your philosophy of music teaching and learning, and your values. As you gain new knowledge and insight into your surroundings, you may find that your pre-conceived ideas and beliefs about music teaching in general and music teaching in your particular school placement may change. This is all part of becoming a reflective music educator.

two
Curriculum and Lesson Planning

FIGURE 2.1. Courtesy of John Morgan.

Just as there are numerous approaches to music teaching and learning, there are multiple ways through which music educators approach lesson and rehearsal planning. Not every cooperating teacher will plan the same way you were taught in your university methods classes. Some may not even appear to follow a written plan. Regardless of what your cooperating teacher seems to use for planning, as a student teacher you have the opportunity to examine existing school and/or district music curriculum to become familiar with the long-term goals designed for each music class and ensemble in your school. Additionally, you can consider the numerous ways in which these curricular goals can be met and assessed through comprehensive lesson and rehearsal plans. The purpose of this chapter is to guide you in the examination of philosophical approaches to music teaching as reflected in curriculum and lesson planning as you become immersed in your student teaching experience.

Philosophy of Music Teaching

Scenario 2.1

Sharon is a student teacher in a high school choral setting. Her cooperating teacher, Mr. Engels, has been teaching for close to 20 years. His program is considered by many to be one of the most successful in the region. His top choir performs frequently at the annual state conference and many of his students are accepted to perform in the all-state chorus. Sharon is excited to work with such a master teacher and is anxious to know what he does on a daily basis to get such fabulous results. After her first week, she is confused. Her university faculty stressed the importance of music literacy and Sharon firmly believes that a choral program that includes the development of sight-singing skills is the key to good musicianship, yet she observes that Mr. Engles' rehearsal routine centers around rote teaching from the piano. The students sing well and are motivated, but the learning process concerns her and she is uncertain what she will take away from this experience.

Discussion

1. Should Sharon be concerned about this approach to teaching?
2. What can Sharon do to optimize her time with Mr. Engles?
3. Do you think Sharon should talk to Mr. Engles about including some sight singing in the rehearsals?
4. What would you do?

Scenario 2.2

Marcus is student teaching in elementary general music with Ms. Flanders, a fourth-year teacher. Marcus was a voice major and always wanted to work with young singers. His goal is to teach in a school where he can teach general music and develop an elementary choral program. When he arrives at Ms. Flanders' room, he sees lots of xylophones and metallaphones, hand drums of various sizes, bins filled with boom whackers and various small percussion instruments, and two rows of 16 electronic keyboards. At the end of his first week, Marcus notes that the children in this program rarely sing. He asks Ms. Flanders if singing is part of her curriculum and she tells him that she was a trumpet major in college and doesn't have much of a singing voice, so she focuses on teaching musical concepts through classroom instruments and keyboards.

Discussion

1. Should Marcus follow Ms. Flanders' curriculum or try to insert his own objectives into the lessons he teaches in her classroom? If you think he should include more singing in his lessons, how should he communicate this to Ms. Flanders?
2. What can Marcus hope to learn in this student teaching experience?

After completing your undergraduate courses, you have probably worked thoughtfully and diligently on developing a teaching philosophy. Although you may realize that your philosophy is a work in progress, you might not see eye to eye with your cooperating teacher on every aspect of music teaching. In fact, you may find yourself in a student teaching placement where you vigorously disagree with how your cooperating teacher handles classroom situations or, in particular, approaches curriculum. For example, some high school music teachers focus on competitions such as solo and ensemble contest, while others collaborate with drama departments to produce musicals. Some music teachers do not have many performances during the school year, whereas others plan their lessons primarily around performances. Some general music teachers adhere strictly to the approaches of Orff, Kodaly, Dalcroze or Gordon, whereas others consider themselves to be eclectic.

Similarly, music teachers vary in their beliefs about musical content and their ultimate goals for their students. Some teachers' primary goal is to identify gifted students and encourage them to continue with formal music instruction, whereas other teachers believe in encouraging all their students to participate in making music regardless of ability. Some teachers want their students to leave with a factual knowledge base about musical styles and genres, whereas others feel their students should experience a variety of music without providing much lecture or context about the music. Some teachers believe that music is the vehicle for reaching children, while others focus on the intrinsic value of music.

Although it is highly unlikely that you will agree with every aspect of your cooperating teacher's philosophical approach to teaching, this is the time in your development as a music teacher for you to be open to understanding the applications of various approaches and learning from them.

Completing worksheet 2.1 will allow you to discover some of your cooperating teacher's thoughts about pedagogy and philosophy.

Worksheet 2.1
Philosophy and Pedagogy

Talk with your cooperating teacher about their philosophical approach to music teaching. In particular, ask the following:

1.   Why do you think music education is important for your students?

2.   What do you wish for your students as a result of participating in your music classes?

3.   Have you been influenced by any particular teaching approach or pedagogy? If so, which one? Why?

4.   How have your beliefs about music education impacted the way in which you plan for instruction?

To Plan or Not to Plan: That is the Question

As you progressed through various music and education methods courses, you likely spent hours agonizing over lesson or unit plans, writing them to fit the particular format provided by your professor or to meet the guidelines found in your class textbook. You probably had philosophical discussions with your classmates and professors regarding the perceived value of detailed planning for music classes or ensembles. In some cases, you may have been required to "script" your lesson plans to indicate precisely what you would say and what questions you might ask to lead your future students to meet your intended educational objectives.

Now that you have entered the world of the music teacher who is to be your mentor for your student teaching experience, you may be concerned that your cooperating teacher's approach to planning is not exactly what you expected or were taught to do. In fact, you may notice that your cooperating teacher seems to "wing it" from the podium or teach primarily from a series book. Keep an open mind so that you may acquaint yourself with your cooperating teacher's approach to music teaching and learning. Consider the following scenarios.

Scenario 2.3

Beth has been at her secondary band student teaching site for three days, observing and carefully taking in everything. She makes notes about the students' abilities, the music they are rehearsing and their daily routines. She notices, however, that Mrs. Dorite, her cooperating teacher, doesn't seem to have a lesson plan book or any notes with her at the podium for any of the ensembles. The only thing resembling a "lesson plan" is a list on the board indicating warm-ups from a method book followed by the titles of the three pieces the band is working on. Beth is confused and concerned because she knows she is required to write detailed lesson plans and work samples for her university supervisor.

Scenario 2.4

Jonathan is approaching the end of his first week in an elementary music student teaching placement. Mr. Hanson, his cooperating teacher, has chosen this day to meet with Jonathan to share his most recent lesson plans and to discuss his expectations for the kind of lesson plans he will require Jonathan to write. Jonathan is taken aback when he sees that Mr. Hanson has used three pages to write one lesson plan for a 30-minute third-grade music class. Jonathan also notices that the plan looks nothing like the kinds of plans he did in his elementary methods class at the university. He starts to worry that he will not be able to live up to Mr. Hanson's expectations.

Discussion

1. What do you think Beth and Jonathan might do in their respective situations? What would you do?
2. Have you encountered anything similar in your student teaching situation? If so, how have you addressed the issues?

Planning With (and Without) Your Cooperating Teacher

Although most university pre-service programs require that you write extensive plans, your involvement with your mentor teacher regarding your role in the planning process will likely vary from placement to placement. It is typically expected that you will ease into the planning and teaching process. Some mentors might ask you to mimic what they do before you actually plan to teach anything on your own. Some will then require you to create and submit your lesson or rehearsal plans well in advance of your actual teaching date, and some will sit with you to cooperatively plan lessons before allowing you to plan on your own.

The plans you are expected to write and maintain for your university may be quite different than what you perceive your cooperating teacher is planning. Although these might differ in format among teacher preparation programs and may, in fact, vary from the type of planning your cooperating teacher does, it is probable that the basic components will be the same. Formats and terminology used may differ from place to place, but basically each lesson or rehearsal plan accounts for the following:

Known: what the students already "know" that is relevant to and necessary for the lesson.

Objectives: sometimes called behavioral objectives, learning objectives, outcomes, or aims, these are the expectations for the students as a direct result of instruction.

Materials: the music literature or songs that will be used in the lesson along with other necessary equipment such as CD player, SmartBoard, ipod, overhead, etc.

Procedures: the steps for achieving the objectives.

Assessment: a plan for determining the extent to which the musical skills and concepts contained in the lesson have been attained.

It is important that you discuss expectations regarding lesson planning with your cooperating teacher as early as possible. Importantly, be sure your cooperating teacher is aware of the lesson plans you are expected to submit to your university supervisor or program. Complete worksheet 2.2 before discussing lesson planning specifics with your cooperating teacher in order to gain an understanding of the way in which your cooperating teacher implements a lesson or rehearsal.

Worksheet 2.2
Lesson Planning

Without asking or looking at your cooperating teacher's plan, observe one full class or rehearsal and list the musical objectives you think your cooperating teacher had in mind. State each as a full objective, using the language and/or wording you were taught in your methods courses.

How can you tell from your observation that these were the objectives of the lesson or rehearsal?

How might these objectives represent a small portion of the larger music curriculum?

From this observation, how can you tell what the students already knew prior to this lesson?

How does your cooperating teacher assess student learning in this lesson?

Cooperating Teacher Discussion
After you complete worksheet 2.2, share your observations and questions about this lesson and lesson planning in general, using the questions below to guide your discussion. Ask your cooperating teacher:

1. What are the expectations of your school administration with regard to lesson plans? Is there a particular format? If so, does it correspond to state or national standards or district curriculum?
2. Are you required to submit lesson plans to your principal? If so, how frequently?
3. How does your daily or periodic assessment of your students impact your planning? How does it impact music grading policies and procedures?

Teaching Without a Plan

Teaching without a plan, or "thinking on your feet," is an important skill. There are times when you may need to abandon your well-thought-out plan for any number of reasons. Perhaps there was a fire drill and you have only 10 minutes of class time left. Perhaps the students really didn't do as well as you thought on the first part of the plan, so moving forward with your plan isn't an option. Or perhaps the students zoomed through your plan and you have 15 minutes remaining before the bell rings (which can be an eternity in a first-grade class!). All of these scenarios require you to think on your feet.

In addition to the cases listed above, it could be that your cooperating teacher suddenly asks you to do something without planning. Aside from those cooperating teachers who plan extensively and expect you to do the same, there are always some cooperating teachers who simply tell you to "teach something next period." They may direct you to the music library, music textbook, district curriculum or scope and sequence, or they may just want you to pick a song or warm up and to decide on your own what to do. In this case, you at least get a chance to mull it over, but you may not have the needed amount of time to actually plan.

Discussion

1. Does your cooperating teacher refer to lesson or rehearsal plans during each lesson?
2. Have you been asked to jump in and teach something without prior notice? If so, was it successful? How prepared did you feel?
3. What sort of direction would you like from your cooperating teacher regarding lesson or rehearsal planning?

Long-Term Planning

In your music methods and education courses, you learned that the objectives of daily lesson or rehearsal plans are typically based on long-term curricular goals. These goals may be derived from national or state arts standards, or built on a district or school music curriculum. Yet as you begin your student teaching experience, you will become immersed in planning portions of lessons or rehearsals, gradually assuming more responsibility for teaching larger sections, then whole lessons or rehearsals. Neither observing your cooperating teacher, nor planning and teaching daily lessons necessarily provides you with information on the broad scope of curricular goals. Understanding the scope of the curriculum, however, is crucial for planning daily lessons.

Cooperating Teacher Discussion
Initiate a discussion with your cooperating teacher regarding the long term goals and curricular outcomes for their music program. Ask your cooperating teacher the following questions:

1. Have you implemented a particular curriculum in this school? Is it district-wide?
2. Does the curriculum adhere to state or national standards?
3. Who determined what the curriculum would be? Was it a collaborative effort of the music teachers in the district, or was it designed by a committee?
4. How do you build daily plans in relation to the school music curriculum?

Assessment and Grading

Scenario 2.5
Sarah has just completed the first half of her student teaching experience working with Mrs. Hanniman, a middle school general–choral teacher. Mrs. Hanniman took her responsibility for student learning very seriously and stressed the importance of monitoring student progress and providing her students with regular written as well as verbal feedback. Mrs. Hanniman helped Sarah create detailed rubrics for every general music unit she planned, thus providing the students with a thorough understanding of expectations for assignments and the basis for grades. Mrs. Hanniman wanted the content, expectations, and grading criteria crystal clear to her students and their parents.

Sarah has now moved on to the second half of her student teaching semester. She is now working with high school choirs under the direction of Mrs. Melford. Sarah has been there for ten days and has seen no evidence of assessment of any form, except for the corrections Mrs. Melford makes from the podium. This makes Sarah wonder how Mrs. Melford will grade students in her choral program.

Discussion

1. Do you think Mrs. Melford will have a basis for grading the choirs?
2. What do you think would be key elements for assessing and grading a high school performing ensemble?

In your methods courses, you were taught the importance of assessment for determining the effectiveness of instruction as well as the progress of your students. Music teachers have a variety of approaches to formative or ongoing assessment. Music worksheets, solo and group performances, class or group presentations, paper and pencil tests, are all examples of items that help teachers assess student progress and plan for instruction. Often scoring rubrics or checklists are used to provide feedback on the quality of student assignments or to keep track of individual student achievements. In some schools, teachers are required to keep track of student progress through the use of a portfolio of student works. Music teachers include recordings or video clips of performances, student compositions, self-assessments and other written works as evidence of students' musical progress.

When it comes to assigning grades, schools or school districts frequently provide guidelines for the kind of grades or comments that will appear on report cards. Music teachers have the daunting and often challenging task of grading students in music classes. Keeping track of the musical achievements of 800 elementary students, for example, can be a nightmare if the teacher is not prepared or organized well in advance of the task. Determining the basis for assigning a grade may be more elusive yet. Should the grade be based on participation? Musical achievement? Musical ability? Good behavior? Is there a distinction between grading music ensembles and music classes?

Worksheet 2.3 involves collecting assessment and grading policies from your student teaching site. After completing worksheet 2.3, discuss your findings with your peers in your seminar or class.

Worksheet 2.3
Assessment

1. How does your cooperating teacher monitor student progress over time?

2. How does your cooperating teacher determine grades for music classes or ensembles?

3. Collect documents pertaining to grading policies and procedures from your student teaching site. List the documents you have collected. Compare and discuss these policies and their relationships to implementation or practicality in music classes or ensembles.

three
Effective Teaching and Rehearsal Techniques

FIGURE 3.1. Courtesy of Rob Lee.

On your path to becoming an effective music educator, you have undoubtedly encountered music educators you consider to be highly effective. In fact, you were likely inspired to become a music educator because of your past experiences with an effective music educator in music classes or ensembles. In this chapter, we will explore some of the traits of highly effective music educators who exemplify positive interactions in the music class that lead to high-quality, often inspirational school music programs.

Discussion

Reflect on a music educator from your past who inspired you to become a music teacher. What characteristics made them an inspirational teacher? As a class, compile a list of traits representing an ideal music educator. You may have done this type of activity when you first began your music education coursework, but as you near your professional goal, your thoughts on effective teaching traits may have evolved or increased. Completing worksheet 3.1 will allow you to reflect on the positive characteristics you possess and the traits you would like to achieve to become an effective music educator.

Worksheet 3.1
Characteristics of an Effective Music Educator

Now that you have had a chance to discuss with your peers the personal characteristics you believe are important for effective music teaching, narrow down those traits to the top ten you most closely associate with an effective, inspirational music educator. Then determine the areas of teaching on which these traits have the most impact, such as facilitating interactions with students, motivating the class, communicating with parents, presenting new concepts, or rehearsing the ensemble.

Trait	Teaching Area Impacted
1.	
2.	
3.	
4.	
5.	
6.	
7.	
8.	
9.	
10.	

Which of these traits do you currently possess?

List your strategies for attaining the remaining characteristics.

Gaining and Maintaining Attention and Interest

Scenario 3.1

Sam is a student teaching intern in general music at an elementary school. The music program there is well regarded and Sam's cooperating teacher is highly respected locally and at the state level. The sixth-grade students typically enter the room to an established routine that involves distributing their music journals and finding their assigned seats while listening to music that is related to the lesson for that day. Following this, the students spend five minutes briefly responding in writing to a journal prompt written on the board. The cooperating teacher monitors their progress by observing, moving around the classroom and offering both non-verbal and verbal encouragement. The routine concludes with a brief discussion of the prompt that segues to a related activity.

Today is to be the first time Sam will teach an entire lesson. He has been watching this routine with interest and decides to stick to it. The students enter to the music Sam selected for the lesson and proceed to pick up their journals and be seated. Much to Sam's dismay, instead of quietly responding to the prompt, they begin to talk to each other. Sam is horrified and stands motionless at the front of the class not knowing what to do.

Discussion

There appears to be something missing from the routine.

- What might be missing from the routine?
- Do you think Sam should have done anything to prevent the chatting?
- What would you have done to regain the students' attention and keep them motivated?

There are multiple approaches to gaining and maintaining student interest. Often music teachers will use established routines to set the tone for the lesson or rehearsal. Some teachers use recorded music while others have prompts, instructions, or the rehearsal order written on the board. Some teachers begin with a question or warm-up routine, while others start with a greeting song. Once the lesson is underway, maintaining student interest and involvement becomes the focal point. This, too, is accomplished effectively through various techniques that above all encourage student participation.

Effective music educators find ways to create an atmosphere in which all students are made to feel like important participants in a musical community. For example, effective music educators involve their students in musical problem-solving. Rather than dictating instructions, effective music educators ask questions that encourage input and foster higher-order thinking skills. Such educators give positive feedback for efforts as well as accomplishments, and provide opportunities for students to find and correct their own errors. Importantly, effective music educators tip the balance of verbal and non-verbal instruction in favor of non-verbal instruction. They use their lesson or rehearsal time efficiently to maximize student participation and music-making.

Worksheet 3.2 will serve as a starting point for a discussion with your peers regarding instructional techniques of highly effective music educators that promote a high level of student participation and interest throughout a lesson or rehearsal.

Worksheet 3.2
Lesson or Rehearsal Engagement

Videotape yourself teaching a lesson or rehearsal segment that you have planned. (Although the camera should be focused entirely on you, be sure to secure the appropriate permissions from your school administration if there is a chance the students will appear on the recording.)

Carefully watch and review your recording to answer the following questions:

1. What was the first thing you said or did to start this portion of the lesson or rehearsal? What was the basis for your choice?

2. How much time (approximately what percentage of the lesson segment) did you spend giving verbal directions? Do you think it was an appropriate amount of verbal direction for this particular segment? How can you tell?

3. Did you modify anything you planned to say or do based on student responses? Describe the changes you made.

4. List any questions you asked the students and their responses. Were there questions that required "yes/no" replies? Questions that assumed the students had certain knowledge base?

5. Did you feel this segment was successful? Why or why not?

Personal Musicianship

Although you have probably learned or observed numerous strategies for rehearsing an ensemble or teaching a musical skill or concept, your personal musicianship skills coupled with a thorough knowledge of musical content is the first step to instructional effectiveness. Your ability to provide effective music instruction must begin by developing and readily modeling your own musicianship skills for your students. Additionally, you must be able to apply those skills to your knowledge and understanding of multiple musical genres and performance mediums common to school music settings.

Cooperating Teacher Discussion
Initiate a discussion with your cooperating teacher regarding the musical skills deemed necessary for effective classroom or rehearsal instruction. Ask your cooperating teacher to share their own educational and musical background that led them to create a successful, musical classroom environment. Reflect on how your own musicianship skills may impact your teaching. Share your findings with your peers in seminar or class.

Monitoring Student Progress and Providing Feedback

Scenario 3.2
Jennifer is student teaching in a high school band setting with Mr. Davis, a music teacher with 15 years of experience. Two weeks into her student teaching, she has become aware that Mr. Davis is a highly skilled musician. He readily plays his trumpet to model phrasing, dynamics, and nuances he expects from his students. Jennifer can hardly believe how quickly he corrects his students' mistakes. It seems he hears every individual in the band as he is conducting. She notices that he is quick to tell students what the mistake is and tell them exactly what the note or rhythm should be and how to finger it. It takes very little time in the rehearsal for him to accomplish this. She begins to worry that she won't be anywhere near as fast as he is and fears that the students won't respect her because of this.

Scenario 3.3

David is student teaching in a high school string program. Mrs. Jenski, his cooperating teacher, has been teaching strings in the same district for ten years. Now in his second week in the school, David begins to realize that the orchestra has far less repertoire than he expected. He notes that Mrs. Jenski stops the group frequently during rehearsals to correct errors, but that she doesn't actually do the correcting. She asks the ensemble if they notice anything wrong at a particular measure or section, and what it might be. She doesn't seem to ever tell them what the problem is. Instead, she asks students to raise their hands if they know what the correct note, rhythm, or bowing might be. David wonders why she doesn't just tell them and get on with the rehearsal. He is also concerned that this process is taking so much of the rehearsal time that the students will never learn their concert repertoire.

Discussion

1. Compare the teaching styles of Mr. Davis and Mrs. Jenski. How are they similar and different?
2. Are Jennifer and David justified in their concerns? Why or why not?
3. Of these two approaches to providing feedback, which appeals to you more? Why?

One of the most important applications of your personal musicianship is the ability to detect errors in music performance. At this point in the process of your pre-service education, you now will need to use your skills as a musician to hear and correct those wrong pitches, rhythms, instrumental fingerings, and/or bowings your students make while singing or playing. Your expertise in identifying those errors proves your musical readiness for teaching. The way in which you correct the errors, however, is at the heart of music teaching and learning. Your attitude toward teaching will undoubtedly influence the strategies you employ in providing appropriate feedback to your students so that they can develop their own independent musicianship skills.

Pacing and Time Management

You already know the importance of determining in advance the amount of time you will allot for each activity or rehearsal segment of a music lesson. Equally important is the speed at which you progress through the lesson, and the ways in which you can minimize the transition time between lesson segments. Consider the amount of musical material your cooperating teacher covers in one lesson, the flow from one segment to the next, and the time spent on each segment.

Cooperating Teacher Discussion

Talk to your cooperating teacher about their strategies for pacing and managing lesson content. Guide your discussion with the following questions:

1. How do you determine how many different components will be in a lesson or rehearsal?
2. How, then, do you determine how much time to spend on each component?
3. What strategies do you use to make the transition from one portion of the lesson to the next?

Effective music educators display both personal and professional characteristics that inspire students to fully participate in music class and to develop their musicianship skills while they develop a lifelong love of music. Such educators know how to motivate and engage their students through the creation of a community of young musicians. Careful reflection on your own personal and professional traits as you progress through your student teaching experience can help you to become that music educator.

four
Creating a
Positive
Learning
Environment

FIGURE 4.1. Courtesy of Dr. Ed Brambley; www.flickr.com/edbrambley.

Knowing your subject matter and preparing lesson plans at the appropriate skill level are only part of the process for successful teaching. Establishing an environment in which students participate as contributing members of a musical community is essential for a successful music program. Classroom management, including the organization of the room, the students, and routine tasks, expectations for student behavior and participation, procedures, rules, and consequences for disciplinary infractions, and a comprehensive knowledge of your student population all contribute to the success of any school music program.

Organizing the Music Classroom

Organization is essential for a well-run music classroom at any level. Organization includes daily tasks such as taking attendance, controlling students entering and exiting the classroom, distributing music, monitoring behavior, and assessing student progress. Organization also includes periodic elements such as submitting grades for report cards, planning a budget, taking inventory of the music library and materials, instrument maintenance and inventory, field trip permissions and transportation, and communicating with parents and administration. Many new teachers are surprised by the amount of time and energy that goes into organization and record keeping. In order to set yourself up for success in student teaching and beyond, it is important for you to be observant of the many organizational facets involved in the management of a school music program. Some of the key components are described below and some components will be addressed in Chapter 5 as we explore the organization of the music program.

Scheduling

Music teachers' schedules are as unique as the buildings in which they teach. For example, district policies on block scheduling, contractual classroom teacher preparation periods, and/or philosophical beliefs about elementary school pull-out instrumental programs all influence the music schedule. Although music teachers may or may not have input regarding their class schedule, the ways in which they organize their time within each class or rehearsal meeting is something that can be controlled. Since music classes or rehearsals vary in length as well as number of contact hours per week, efficient time use is essential to the overall management of a music program.

A typical school day is often filled with disruptions to the school schedule. Field trips will occur and school assemblies happen. It is important to remain as flexible as possible when you encounter these changes. Remember that as a music teacher you may very well need the assistance of your colleagues and administrators when you are planning your events. Make sure you are aware of upcoming events and plan for the changes in schedule in order to use class time as efficiently as possible.

Record Keeping

As a student teacher it is imperative that you assist your cooperating teacher with the daily and long-range organization of records. Most likely there is a procedure for daily items such as attendance, students entering and exiting the classroom, and for common occurrences such as students using the bathroom, and visiting the nurse or administration. In most schools, there is a "pass" the students must carry when out of the room. Make sure you are familiar with these procedures and that you follow them when you are the lead instructor. To help you with this, complete worksheet 4.1.

Worksheet 4.1
Record Keeping

Complete this worksheet on your own.

Using your observation skill and knowledge of the classroom, answer the following questions:

1. List the daily record-keeping activities you observe that are required of your cooperating teacher.

2. List the period or long-term record-keeping activities that are evident in your cooperating teacher's classroom or office or through your observations or prior conversations.

3. Determine whether or not there is a school or district policy regarding any of these items.

4. How, if at all, do the daily record-keeping tasks relate to the periodic tasks in this school?

Cooperating Teacher Discussion

1. What single daily record-keeping activity takes the most amount of time?
2. Are there any tricks to staying on top of the daily record-keeping tasks? Are there any tricks to staying on top of the occasional or periodic tasks?
3. Did they feel prepared as a new teacher for the various kinds of record keeping?
4. Have they had difficulty with a particular aspect of record keeping in the past? If so, how has it been resolved?

■   Offer to assist your cooperating teacher with some of the daily record-keeping tasks.

■   Ask your cooperating teacher if there are particular tasks that you can create a records system to assist with.

Individual school districts or buildings have varying requirements for lesson planning and assessment of students. Some buildings require that a formal lesson plan for each lesson taught is available for inspection by administration. Other schools may allow for more flexibility in the way lesson plans are constructed or maintained. Speak with your cooperating teacher about the expectations for their school building and be sure that you follow common procedure through out your student teaching.

You may also play a role in long-range record keeping, such as the use of school instruments and materials, the planning and preparation for field trips, communication with parents and booster organizations, fundraising, and concert planning. Be sure to talk about these procedures with your cooperating teacher and volunteer to assist them as they plan for larger events. Most record keeping associated with field trips and transportation are regulated by the individual school district or building. Other long-range records and organization may be created and regulated by your cooperating teacher, such as materials, uniform, and instrument control, issues related to booster clubs, the music library, and fundraising. It is important to know as many of these organization procedures as possible. You may wish to request sample copies of these records for later consideration when you are constructing your own music program.

FIGURE 4.2. Courtesy of Army.mil Web Team.

Building Positive Relationships

Scenario 4.1

Sam is fulfilling this portion of his student teaching experience working with beginning strings. Johnny, a fifth-grade string player, has left his instrument at home. Sam gives him a verbal warning, allows Johnny to use a school instrument for the day, and sends a note home to Johnny's parents acknowledging his lack of responsibility. Johnny is instructed to take the note home, have his parents sign it, and return it to school during the next rehearsal. Johnny comes to the next rehearsal, once again without his instrument and without the note. Sam sends the note home once more, this time with a stern handwritten addition indicating how this might impact Johnny's grade. The next day Sam is summoned to the principal's office because the parents have complained that the student teacher is harassing the child.

Discussion

1. How do you think the student teacher communicated expectations to the parents prior to this incident?
2. What kind of conversation do you believe the principal will have with the student teacher?
3. How might this impact Johnny's future behavior in string class and his relationship with the student teacher?
4. Why might Johnny forget to bring his instrument to school?
5. What role do you think Sam's cooperating teacher should have played in this instance?

In order to create a positive learning environment, you must first create a positive student–teacher relationship. You may be working within an environment where students participate fully with few, if any, disruptions. Consider that it is most likely that the cooperating teacher has done a lot of hard work to establish this kind of environment. A large contributing factor to the rehearsal flow may have been in establishing a positive rapport with their students. You are less likely to have behavioral problems when you, as the teacher, provide an environment based on collaboration and mutual support. Planning for effective instruction involves developing and implementing a classroom management plan that is based to a certain extent on your knowledge of the students both collectively and individually. When you are observing your cooperating teacher, pay special attention to the ways in which they interact with students. Use worksheet 4.2 to guide your observations.

Worksheet 4.2
Observing Teacher–Student Interactions

As you observe your cooperating teacher's daily interactions with students, make note of the following:

Rapport
What do you think contributes to the relationship between your cooperating teacher and their students?

Use of Humor
How does your cooperating teacher insert humor into lessons or discussions with students either formally (from the podium, for example) or informally (talking to individual students while exiting the classroom, for example)?

Proximity to Students
From where in the classroom or rehearsal hall does your cooperating teacher deliver instruction? Are the interactions stationary or does your cooperating teacher move about the room?

Decision-Making Involvement
How does your cooperating teacher involve students in everyday decisions? Are the students given opportunities to solve problems or resolve issues? Do the students have input or involvement in record-keeping tasks such as taking attendance?

Cooperating Teacher Discussion
Discuss the following questions with your cooperating teacher:

1. When do you think it is appropriate to use humor in teaching?
2. Is there ever a time when humor may be offensive or inappropriate?
3. Is it ok to be serious?
4. Is it better to move about the classroom during instruction or to remain more or less in one place? Why?
5. To what extent do you feel students should be involved in everyday decision-making? What strategies do you use to involve students? How are these communicated to students?
6. What have you purposely done to develop and maintain a positive relationship with your students?

Building positive relationships with your students is paramount for establishing a climate that allows for well-managed rehearsals and lessons. Developing such positive relationships will also contribute to your lifelong enjoyment of teaching. There are several small ways in which you can begin to establish positive relationships with your students. A few strategies are listed below:

- *Learn their names.* Use nametags or seating charts to learn individual students' names as quickly as possible. Ensure that they always address you by the proper title, such as Mr. or Ms. to maintain mutual respect.
- *Avoid confrontations with students.* Discuss problems you may encounter in a one-on-one situation outside of class to avoid possible embarrassment to the student and to give yourself time to choose your words.
- *Maintain self-control.* When handling discipline matters, remain in control of your feelings. Try not to take student misbehavior personally.
- *Allow for student input.* Whenever possible, allow students to share in decision-making processes, such as the creation of classroom rules and consequences, musical decisions within a rehearsal or class session, the selection of some musical materials when appropriate, and in resolving their own behavioral issues.
- *Meaningful feedback.* Students respond best when they receive accurate feedback, both constructive and positive. Deliberately negative feedback should be avoided or stated in a meaningfully constructive way.

Discussion

1. Describe an incident you have either witnessed or been involved in where a disciplinary action was avoided due to positive relationships.
2. In your opinion, what do you feel are the most important skills, activities, or other preventive measures a music teacher should take to avoid behavioral issues?
3. In your opinion, what actions can be detrimental to creating positive relationships with students?

Knowing Your Students

Classrooms are microcosms of the population as a whole. Your classroom and school community is as diverse as the community surrounding the school. Exploring the larger community may help you to understand the diverse backgrounds of the students within your classroom, such as customs and cultures, ethnicity, religion, language, and socioeconomic status.

You must also acknowledge diversity issues relevant to schooling such as learning styles, academic ability, musical skills, and mental, physical, or behavioral disabilities. At times you may need to consider how students' home and living conditions, such as any turmoil within the home, major life changes, recent moves, and relationships with family or friends may impact on their performance in school. It is a careful balancing act to be respectful of student privacy while using what you know in order to best serve student needs. For more information on ethics and legal issues see Chapter 7.

The students with whom you are working are as different as the people you have known through out your life. While in your private life you have the freedom to select whom you befriend, within the classroom you are the teacher and therefore must interact equally with all of your students. This is not to say that expectations for student behavior should vary greatly based on individual factors, it merely means that knowing your students well will help you to determine the best approach to create a positive learning environment.

As you read the scenario below, consider your role as a student teaching in a well-established learning environment.

Scenario 4.2

Becky Johnson's cooperating teacher, Mr. Adams, recently informed her that the high school band will be attending a regional festival the following week and he will not be present for the middle school band rehearsals. He would like Becky to run the entire middle school band rehearsal in his absence, since there will only be a non-music substitute teacher in the room. Becky is excited about running the rehearsal on her own and is eager to test her skills as the lead teacher in the room.

As the bell rings to start Becky's first solo teaching experience, she decides that instead of greeting students at the door as Mr. Adams typically does, she will spend those extra moments reviewing her detailed rehearsal plan. When she approaches the podium, she realizes that some students are not in their correct seats. She kindly asks the ensemble members to move back to their assigned seats. As they move, she hears some students grumble that they don't feel like playing today. In the back of the room, a few members of the percussion section take a seat on the floor and begin to share trading cards with one another. She once again asks that all students move to their correct playing positions. Begrudgingly they begin to move while continuing to talk to one another.

She directs their attention to a rhythmic pattern she has put on the board and, despite their continuous talking, she begins to conduct the pattern. Only a few students attempt to play the pattern. She stops the ensemble, describes the rhythm pattern for them, and begins to conduct again. While a few more students begin to play, several others continue to talk over her. As Becky's frustration builds, she once again stops the ensemble and begins to model the pattern for the students. Simultaneously, a trombone player removes his mouthpiece and begins to blow rude buzzing sounds in the pattern of the rhythm on the board. The class breaks down into a fit of laughter. Becky feels defeated.

Discussion

1. What were the primary issues that encouraged the students to behave as they did?
2. Why did the disruptions in the rehearsal continue?
3. If you were in Becky's situation, what would you do next?
4. How could this situation have been avoided?

Scenario 4.3

After stepping off the podium for a moment to regain her composure, Becky, noticeably upset, attempts to continue with her middle school band rehearsal. She directs the students once again to play the rhythm pattern on the board. Once more, the trombone player removes his mouthpiece and starts to buzz. This time he stands and mimics Becky, but plays arbitrary patterns repeatedly. Becky becomes infuriated. She leaves the podium and approaches the student to grab the mouthpiece from his hands. In the process, the trombone falls to the floor and the bell is dented. The trombone player starts screaming at Becky for damaging his instrument and begins to push and shove Becky away. The substitute teacher rushes to the phone and calls security for assistance. Security arrives and removes the student from the classroom. The class finally becomes silent. Visibly shaken, Becky attempts to carry on with rehearsal but little is accomplished.

At the end of the school day, Becky is called into the principal's office to explain what happened in class that day. The principal tells her that a meeting with the trombone player's parents has been set for the following morning.

Discussion

1. Why do you think the situation escalated so quickly?
2. Was it necessary to call security? Why or why not?
3. How might Becky prepare for the meeting with the student's parents?

Creating a Management Plan

As a student teacher, you are entering a classroom filled with numerous predetermined expectations for student participation and behavior. These expectations come from a variety of sources. Often there is a district and/or school-wide "code of conduct" or "handbook" that is distributed to students and parents each year. Sometimes there are additional classroom policies and procedures constructed by your cooperating teacher. While many of the district, school-wide and teacher-constructed policies can be made available to you, you may have to use your keen sense of observation coupled with deliberate conversations with your cooperating teacher to fully understand the expectations for students in your specific music classrooms.

Previously in Chapter 1, you observed your classroom teaching environment (see worksheet 1.4). The organization within the physical space in your classrooms is intentional. By re-examining these spaces in terms of student expectations you may gain a broader understanding of behavioral expectations of students.

Classrooms range upon a continuum from highly structured to extremely flexible. Your cooperating teacher has already determined the level at which they prefer their classroom to function, whether it be through perfectly aligned rows of chairs or space available for open seating. In the music classroom, these are sometimes telltale signs for the behavioral expectations of students. Complete worksheet 4.3 to guide your exploration of classroom expectations.

Worksheet 4.3
Management of Physical Teaching Space

Using your knowledge of the classroom, answer the following questions:

1. How are materials organized within the classroom space?

2. How are students organized within the classroom space?

3. Are students assigned a specific seating order? If so, what is that order and how is it determined?

---

4. What is the policy for entering and exiting the classroom at the beginning and end of the class session?

5. What are the expectations for students' personal belongings within the classroom space?

6. Are rules, behavioral expectations, or consequences displayed within the classroom?

Cooperating Teacher Discussion

1. What are the rules or expectations for student behavior in your classroom?
2. How were these rules or expectations created?
3. How are these rules or expectations expressed to students?
4. What are the consequences when a rule or expectation is broken?
5. Are the consequences aligned with district or school policy?

Reflection

Using information from this worksheet, begin to construct a one to two-page classroom management plan. This plan should include examples of rules you intend to use in your future classroom, a brief explanation of why and/or how the rules were created, and the consequences for breaking stated rules or rewards for good behavior.

Classroom rules and expectations, along with the consequences for breaking the rules, are a primary means for maintaining a positive learning environment. It is of utmost importance that your students are well aware of the rules, expectations, and consequences prior to any disciplinary action. Two of the greatest mistakes that new teachers make in terms of classroom management are: 1) being unclear with students about the rules and expectations for behavior; and 2) being inconsistent in following the predetermined consequences when rules are broken.

In scenarios 4.2 and 4.3, Becky struggled with the clarity of establishing expectations and consistency in consequences. From the very start of class she avoided the typical routine of meeting students at the door as they entered the classroom. There is no doubt that the students would have been aware that there would be differences in teaching between Becky and Mr. Adams, but Becky clearly reminded them of this by straying from the established routine. Once class was started, Becky allowed for the talkative and disruptive behaviors, which most likely would not have been tolerated by her cooperating teacher to continue. Instead of addressing the issue head on and establishing higher expectations, she decided to ignore the situation and stick with her lesson plan. To make matters worse, she had not established consequences for poor behavior. When behavior had elevated to an extreme level, she had no rational means for control or punishment. Becky clearly made both mistakes common of new teachers. Her behavior was reactive instead of proactive.

Rules and expectations for behavior are present in every music classroom. Some teachers may have very clearly defined rules that could even be posted in a highly visible area of the classroom, while others may have rules that are less easy to determine, but are none the less active. As a student teacher, understanding the expectations for student behavior in your classroom is imperative. If the rules are not posted, you must speak with your cooperating teacher to determine their expectations. It can be difficult at first to follow rules and expectations that you have not personally created, but you must trust the experience of your cooperating teacher, after all you are a guest in their classroom. Even if you disagree with the set rules or consequences that are established, you must follow the preset expectations. There must be consistency between your cooperating teacher's expectations and your own. Student behavior will break down if there are issues with consistency.

Dangerous Behaviors

While a management plan can account for typical situations, there are actions that go beyond normal classroom behavior. You must check with your cooperating teacher and school policy to ensure you know how to handle possible dangerous behavior. Worksheet 4.4 will help guide a conversation between you and your cooperating teacher regarding dangerous behaviors.

Worksheet 4.4
Dangerous Behaviors

This worksheet is to be completed with the assistance of your cooperating teacher. Discuss each of the following questions with your cooperating teacher to build a better understanding of possible dangerous behaviors that can occur within the classroom or the school building and how you might best handle these situations.

1. Have you ever experienced or witnessed any acts of violence within your classroom or elsewhere within the school building? If so, can you please describe the incident and how you or another teacher reacted in that situation?
2. Did this experience affect your classroom management plan, including rules, expectations or consequences?
3. What should I do if I experience or witness an act of violence on school property?

Discuss the following issues with your cooperating teacher and use the space provided below to take notes on your conversation:

- Inappropriate sexual behavior
- Truancy
- Drug use
- Weapons
- Fighting/violent behavior
- Bullying or threatening

Notes

When an Incident Occurs

When behavioral issues are consistently an issue, it is a good idea to ensure you are documenting the situation. An easy way to do this during class time is to keep track of occurrences on an attendance sheet or seating chart. If behavioral issues remain constant with a particular student, you may want to keep a journal of your interactions so that you have a record of how issues have been handled over time. When journaling, it is important to note the date, the nature of the disruption, how the disruption was handled, and any consequences or punishments that were distributed. If you have clearly stated rules and expectations for behavior coupled with known consequences, it will make record keeping much easier.

It is not uncommon to encounter a particular student who is having reoccurring incidents. If you find a student that is having a difficult time following the rules or has progressed through the most basic of consequences, it is time to consider both journaling about the incidents and beginning communication with other teachers, councilors, and administrators. Communication about the student should be handled in a professional way that respects the student's individual right to privacy. School counselors and administrators may be able to assist you in understanding individual students for whom behavior may be a problem.

If a student is a consistent disruption or if their behavior is violent, you will want to contact administration or school security immediately. Some school buildings have policies regarding poor student behavior beyond the typical. It is imperative that you follow all guidelines and policies and that you are in communication with administrators about how you are interacting with the disruptive student.

Some incidents may require that you contact the parents about their child's behavior. This should only be done after you have communicated with your school administrator. Contacting parents regarding behavior issues can often result in the parents contacting administration, and it is much easier on you in the long run if your administrators are fully aware of the situation before they receive a phone call from angry parents.

Discussion

1. What kinds of behaviors do you feel a teacher can control within their classroom and what kinds of behaviors do you feel warrant communication with school counselors or administration?
2. At what point should a teacher contact a disruptive student's parents?
3. How do you feel a teacher should begin a discussion about a disruptive student's behavior with their parents?
4. What are the possible difficulties a music teacher can encounter when dealing with a consistently disruptive student?
5. Have you had any experiences with a consistently disruptive student? How have you handled the situation?

five
Program
Organization

FIGURE 5.1. Courtesy of Dave Hogg.

Introduction

Each music program is unique in size, structure, and emphasis, but there are many similarities regarding program organization. Regardless of whether you are teaching elementary general music to a multitude of younger students or running a secondary level choral, instrumental or general music program with older students, you will need to organize your program. Organization provides structure and, in the long run, leads to less stress for you and more time for planning activities for your students. The more time you spend during your student teaching experience investigating the organizational systems your cooperating teacher(s) use, the better prepared you will be for your first teaching position.

As you are most likely discovering, much of the music teaching profession is based on materials, paperwork, and communication, all of which require a high level of organization. It's not uncommon for music teachers to spend a large portion of the working day organizing their program. At all levels, there are concerts or field trips to organize and instruments, uniforms, and music to purchase and maintain. There may also be parent organizations that require communication or leadership. In districts or schools where music is not compulsory, you will need to advocate for music education, recruit student enrollment and plan for issues related to retaining the students you already have. Additionally, you will need to create and plan for activities that cross curricular lines, including integration of the curriculum and collaboration with others at your school building or within the school district.

This section of the textbook is a series of online worksheets that will guide your investigation of the organizational structures that are currently in place in your student teaching environment(s). Each worksheet can be repeated multiple times for each location in which you are working. It is important that you explore various organizational systems, as there are differences based on the specific needs of each program. For example, the budget at an elementary school may differ from one at a secondary school. At the elementary level you may have less library materials than at the secondary level, but you may have more collaboration with teachers outside the music classroom. At all levels you may need to have communication with parent organizations. At the elementary level this may be a local Parent, Teacher and Student Organization, whereas at the secondary level you may have a choir, orchestra, or band Boosters organization.

Worksheet 5.1
Budgeting

Organization of your school music program's budget can be a daunting task. Use this worksheet to investigate how your cooperating teachers plan their yearly budget.

School Name:
Description of Music Program (elementary general, high school chorus, etc):

Discuss the following questions with cooperating teacher:

1. When is your budget due and to whom do you submit it?
2. What is your role in planning your program's budgetary needs?
3. Do you have assistance from your school's administration, school district (or district music supervisor), or other outside agencies?
4. How far in advance do you need to schedule your budgetary needs?
5. When is your budget due and to whom?
6. What elements does your budget consist of?
7. Do you need to plan and pay for the following?

   a. Instruments purchases, repairs and maintenance
   b. Uniform purchases, maintenance, and cleaning
   c. Musical scores and musical materials
   d. Photocopying
   e. Concert venues
   f. Festivals and competitions
   g. Transportation
   h. Classroom decorations and materials
   i. Publicity and advertising
   j. Field trips or off campus events
   k. Other elements not listed above

8. How much input do you have in the amount of funds you require or are requesting?
9. Do you ever have issues with funding requests?
10. Once you have received funds, how do access them?
11. Who within your school building or district controls your funding?
12. Do you receive any funding (or grants) from outside your school building or district?
13. Is there access to additional funding once the budgets have been set?

    a. Who do you ask for funding should unplanned events occur?
    b. What is the likelihood of receiving additional funds once the school year begins?

Ask your cooperating teacher for a copy of a current or past budget for their program and attach it to this worksheet.

Worksheet 5.2
Field and Off-Campus Trips

Planning for field and off-campus trips requires a tremendous amount of paperwork. When you leave campus with students, you are dealing with issues of
budgeting, transportation, permissions, and class coverage.

School Name:
Description of Music Program (elementary general, high school band, etc):

Discuss the following questions with your cooperating teacher:

1. How often do you take students off campus?
2. What groups of students do you take off campus most frequently?
3. What are the reasons for taking groups of students off campus?
4. In general, is the school or district administration supportive of off-
    campus activities?
5. Are students ever financially responsible for trip-related costs?
6. Do you ever travel outside the state or internationally? Are there any
    differences in planning for these kinds of trips? If so, what are the
    differences?
7. When you take a group of students off campus, how do you plan and
    prepare class coverage for those who do not attend the trip?

Please list the required paperwork for taking students off campus along with
to whom the materials are due and the estimated timelines in the table below.
In the "Estimated Due Date" column, list the approximate number of
weeks or months that these materials must be submitted to administration or
sent home to parents/guardians. Assume that this is a "typical" trip to a local
festival or performance. Add additional lines for duties not included in the
list below.

Administrative Duty	Estimated Due Date	To Whom Materials Are Due
Budget Request for Trip		
Transportation Request		
Information About the Trip to Parents		
Consent Forms to Parents		
Request for Chaperones		
Request for Class Coverage		
Other:		

- Ask your cooperating teacher to share any stories they have or know about field or off-campus trips that did not go as planned. These stories can be from their own experience or the experiences of other teachers.
- Offer to assist your cooperating teacher with the required paperwork for any up coming field or off-campus trips.
- Gather sample letters, forms, and other paperwork that are used in this program for your own future reference.

Worksheet 5.3
Instrument Purchasing and Maintenance

Regardless of the setting, the music program you are working in is likely to have and use instruments. While they may be highly prevalent in an instrumental setting, general and choral settings most likely have a piano, keyboard, or some other kind of classroom instrument.

School Name:
Description of Music Program (elementary general, high school band, etc):

Using your familiarity with the classroom environment, briefly list the instruments used in the music classroom. If you are in an instrumental setting, you may list instruments family names and the estimated number of instruments.

Discuss the following questions with your cooperating teacher:

1. How were the classroom instruments purchased? What source of funding was used?
2. Do you have an annual budget for the purchasing of new instruments?
a. If so, how do you place the request to purchase new instruments?
b. If not, what channels must you go through to request the purchase of new instruments?
3. How are the instruments organized and categorized?
4. Is there a listing of instruments either in the classroom or in the larger school building or district?
5. How are instruments secured or safeguarded?
6. What is the procedure when an instrument is damaged or lost?
7. Is there an annual budget for the maintenance or repair of instruments?

   a. If so, what is the annual budget and what kinds of repairs or maintenance can be covered from these funds?
   b. If not, how do you request financial assistance to cover repairs for maintenance?

■   If the program has an instrument library or instrument inventory, please attach a copy to this worksheet.
■   If the program has an instrument purchase, repair or maintenance budget please attach a copy to this worksheet.

Worksheet 5.4
Integrating the Curriculum and Collaboration

Many music teachers work in collaboration with both music teachers and other teachers in their building or district. On occasion, music teachers are asked to integrate musical concepts, themes, ideas, and materials outside the music classroom. An example of this may be a school-wide event or theme, such as a fifth-grade focus on American History, or a middle school choir performance at a theme-based school assembly. This worksheet is divided into two sections based on the most common forms of curricular integration and collaboration.

School Name:
Description of Music Program (elementary general, high school band, etc):

Integrating the Curriculum and Collaboration with Non-Music Teachers

1.   What evidence have you seen in regards to curriculum integration in this music program?

2.   Describe the integration below.

Discuss the following questions with your cooperating teacher:

1.   Have you been approached by teachers in other curricular fields to suggest musical materials that would correspond with those teachers' subject area?

  a. If so, what kinds of materials were you able to provide them?

2.   Have you ever participated in a school-wide curricular project, program, or public performance that had a direct impact on the materials you used in the music classroom?

  a. If so, what was the project and how did it affect the music curriculum?

Collaboration with Other Music Teachers

1. Based on your experiences in this setting, does your cooperating teacher appear to have a professional relationship with other music teachers?
a. If so, who are these teachers and why is there the need for a relationship?

2. Brainstorm a list of reasons why you may need to have professional relationships with other music teachers.

Discuss the following questions with your cooperating teacher:

1. Do you work particularly close with other music teachers?
2. What kind of professional relationship do you have with them?
3. How do these relationships affect your planning, preparation, activities, and overall music teaching?

Worksheet 5.5
Music and Materials Library

Keeping musical scores and materials organized is a must for the success of a music program over time. Some programs have relatively new libraries, while others may be decades old. In addition, there may be musical libraries, materials, and resources outside the school building.

School Name:
Description of Music Program (elementary general, high school band, etc):

Complete the following tasks on your own.

1. If the program has a music library or collection of resources, investigate where it is housed and who has access to this space. List your findings below.

2. Describe, in detail, how the music library or collection of resources is organized. Be sure to list each main organization category. For example, in a choral music library, it may be organized by secular and sacred then by voice part, whereas in a general music setting they might be organized by activity or grade level.

3. Are musical recordings or videos part of this library or collection?

Discuss the following questions with your cooperating teacher:

1. Did you organize the musical library or materials collection or was it organized when you took this position?
2. How is the library or materials collection maintained?
3. Do you have assistance in keeping the library or collection organized?

4. Do other music educators ask to use materials from this library or collection?

    a. If so, what records to you maintain to ensure you know the whereabouts of musical scores or materials?

5. Are there any music libraries or musical collections located outside the school building that you have access to?

    a. If so, where are these located and how to you gain access?

6. When new scores or materials are purchased, what is the process for adding them to the library or collection?

7. Do you have any music scores or materials that you have purchased with your personal funds that are housed in the library or collection?

Additional activities:

■ Do a scavenger hunt to find the oldest or newest score in the musical library or collection.

■ Offer to assist your cooperating teacher in maintaining the music library or materials collection.

Worksheet 5.6
Parent Organizations and Support

Parent organizations, both music specific and non-music specific, can offer a tremendous amount of support to any music program. They can help with daily tasks or larger projects, as well as advocate for your music program. Occasionally, they can be a source of financial assistance.

School Name:
Description of Music Program (elementary band, high school chorus, etc):

Discuss the following questions with your cooperating teacher:

1. Do you have a specific music parent organization for this program?

    a. If so, please answer the following questions:

        i.   How do they assist you, and in what music program activities are they involved?
        ii. How often do you ask for support from this organization?
        iii. How do you communicate with this organization?
        iv. Does this organization assist your program financially, and if so, are these funds separate from general school funds?
        v.   Did you begin this organization or was it in place when you began teaching in this program?
        vi. Do you have any words of advice in starting or maintaining a parents organization?

2. Do you seek assistance from any non-music specific parent organizations at the school building or district?

    a. If so, please answer the following questions:

        i.   How do they assist you, and what music program activities are they involved?
        ii. How often do you ask for support from this organization?
        iii. How do you communicate with this organization?
        iv. Does this organization assist your program financially, and if so, are these funds separate than general school funds?
        v.   Do you have any words of advice in starting or maintaining a relationship with a non-music specific parents organization?

3. What are the keys to success in working with any parent organization?

4. Would you suggest that a new music teacher organize a music-specific parent organization when they begin their first teaching position?
5. In your opinion, is a music-specific parent organization a good idea at all teaching levels or any music teaching program?
6. From your experience as a music teacher or from stories you have heard from others, what difficulties may a music teacher have in starting or maintaining a parent organization?

    a. If so, how can such difficult situations be avoided?

Additional activities:

- Attend a meeting of the music parents or general parents' organization.
- In preparation of your first year of teaching, write a letter of introduction asking parents to start and join a newly organized music parent organization.

Worksheet 5.7
Performance Planning

Performance is the primary way in which we share the activities that occur in the music classroom. Many elements go into the planning and preparation for performances. This worksheet will guide you through the process of planning for on campus performances.

School Name:
Description of Music Program (elementary band, high school chorus, etc):

Discuss the following questions with your cooperating teacher:

1. How many on-campus performances do each of your ensembles or classes present in a typical academic year?
2. How far in advance do you begin planning performances and what is your general thought process for planning when to have a performance?
3. Typically, do your performances include only students within your music classes, or do you combine performances to include multiple musical groups or ensembles, such as a joint concert between bands, choirs, and orchestras or elementary general music classes and elementary orchestra?
4. What elements go into the planning of and preparation for on-campus performances? Be sure to discuss the following:

   a. Uniforms and dress/appearance
   b. Communication with administration
   c. Reservation of the performance venue for dress rehearsals and performance
   d. Communication with parents and students
   e. Organization of the performance venue and who is responsible for set up
   f. Cost for admission, if any
   g. Creation and printing of the concert program
   h. Any other issues

5. How do you advertise your on campus performances?

Additional activities:

- Offer to assist your cooperating teacher with any planning or preparation for an upcoming performance.
- Create a concert program for an upcoming performance.
- Create a letter to communicate an upcoming performance to parents and students.
- Create the publicity materials for an up coming performance.

Worksheet 5.8
Publicity and Advocacy

Publicizing your music program and advocating for continuance or even growth, of school music, is important for all music educators. Use this worksheet to develop a plan of action for gathering support for your future music program.

School Name:
Description of Music Program (elementary band, high school chorus, etc):

Discuss the following questions with your cooperating teacher:.

1. How do you advertise for the music program within the school building? How do you advertise for the music program outside the school building?
2. Have you ever gone to the school board, parent organizations, or other outside agencies to speak about the importance of music in the schools?
3. Do you feel it is important for music educators to deliberately advocate for music education, or do you feel that quality public performance is enough?
4. In regards to your answers to the above questions, do you feel well supported in your school building, school district, and community?

Please complete the following on your own.

- Create a brief statement about the importance of music education in general or specific to the program you are currently working in, and ask to share that statement via the parent newsletter, school newspaper, or daily announcements.
- Write a one-page "plan of action" that highlights how you will be advocate for school music programs in your future teaching position.
- Create a small advertisement for music education in general and attempt to get this published in a local newspaper or community resource.
- Search for online resources that show or state the importance of music education in the schools and keep an ongoing list of these resources.

Worksheet 5.9
Recruitment

In schools or programs where music is not compulsory, you will need to recruit students to participate. This worksheet will guide you through consideration when recruiting students into a school music program.

School Name:
Description of Music Program (elementary band, high school chorus, etc):

Discuss the following questions with your cooperating teacher:

1. How do you recruit students into this program?
2. Are students able to join at any time during their academic career or are they only admitted at certain times?
3. What kinds of experiences do students need to have had prior to enrolling in the music classes or ensembles offered?
4. Is there a particular music recruitment event that takes place at a certain time of year?

    a. If so, is this related to students transitioning from one age level to another or is it independent to age level?

5. Can students join your classes at any time during the school year?
6. Do you communicate musical offerings with parents?
7. How are new students that meet the pre-established criteria for participation found in the school building?

Please complete the following on your own.

- Offer to assist your cooperating teacher in the planning and preparation of recruitment events.
- Draft a letter of introduction to either the music program you are currently working with or what you imagine will be your first teaching position and share this draft with your cooperating teacher. Be sure to highlight the benefits of participation as well as the required skills for participation.
- If no formal recruitment event occurs in your current student teaching placement, draft a few ideas that could be of assistance to your cooperating teacher should they elect to start one.

Worksheet 5.10
Retention and Student Leadership

School Name:
Description of Music Program (elementary band, high school chorus, etc):

Discuss the following questions with your cooperating teacher:

1. What do you believe are the strongest motivations for students to stay involved in this music program?
2. What do you believe are the greatest challenges facing students to continue participation?

Please complete the following on your own.

1. Using your powers of observation, explore possible reasons why students may elect not to continue in this program.
2. Evaluate the mechanisms your teacher uses to retain students in their program. Pay close attention to the following:

    a. Seat or chair positions
    b. Section of ensemble leadership positions
    c. Awards
    d. Recognition
    e. Classroom environment
    f. Select ensembles
    g. If you are unable to find surface-based retention mechanisms, what other elements may be in place at a deeper level?

3. If leadership positions are given to students, how does this process work? Is it based on student-run elections or does the teacher decide?
4. In your opinion, what are the strengths of having student leaders and what are the foreseeable difficulties?

Please complete the following on your own.

■   If you were to decide that you would like to have student leaders, what system would you use for nominating or electing them?
■   Name three specific ways in which you could encourage students to remain in music classes and briefly describe these below.

Worksheet 5.11
Uniforms

It is common for ensembles and music classes to either have a formal uniform or a suggested dress code for performances. This worksheet will guide a conversation with your cooperating teacher regarding the purchasing and maintaining of uniforms, as well as communication with students and parents about uniform use.

School Name:
Description of Music Program (elementary band, high school marching band, etc):

Discuss the following questions with your cooperating teacher:

1. Are uniforms required for performance?

    a. If so, are students required to purchase their uniforms or are they supplied by the school?
    b. If not, is there a suggested dress code for performances?

2. How are uniforms or concert dress expectations communicated with parents or guardians?
3. Is the school building or district administration supportive of the uniform or concert dress policy?
4. If uniforms are provided by the school, please answer the following questions.

    a. How are uniforms budgeted for and how do you make a request for new uniforms?
    b. What systems are in place for loaning uniforms to students?
    c. What happens if a uniform is lost or damaged?
    d. Is there a budget for uniform maintenance? If so, what is this budget used for?
    e. Are uniforms cleaned regularly? If so, who is responsible for uniform cleaning?

5. If parents or guardians are required to purchase uniforms, how is this communicated?

    a. Do you have relationships with local uniform vendors?

    b. What happens if a child can not afford a required performance uniform?

6. If you do not use formal uniforms, but set forth expectations for student dress, how is this communicated with parents or guardians?

    a. Are there consequences for not meeting performance dress expectations? If so, what are they?

7. In your opinion, what is the most difficult or time-consuming aspect of uniforms or concert dress?

Please complete the following on your own.

- If your program uses uniforms, explore the in-place systems for their care and maintenance, including how they are distributed to students or purchased by students.
- If your program uses performance dress code expectations, explore how this is communicated to parents or guardians.

six
Seeking Employment

FIGURE 6.1. Courtesy of Eastern Washington University 2009.

Throughout your student teaching experience, it is important for you to be planning ahead with regards to what will be required of you to find employment as a music educator. Many of the tasks involved in seeking and gaining employment take a significant amount of time and effort to construct. Every step of the process requires reflecting thoughtfully on your teaching and prior experiences, professionalism in your writing skills and verbal communication, thoroughness in preparation, and practice in putting all of these skills and elements together. Seeking employment is challenging and time consuming. You must begin planning for this process as soon as possible as waiting until jobs become available is too late to put together a solid package of materials. In order to assist you with this process, this chapter will focus on the creation of resumes, portfolios, finding employment opportunities, contact with potential employers, applications and interviews.

Professionalism

Professionalism in relation to seeking employment can be defined as presenting high-quality products, having impressive competencies in a particular set of skills, communicating effectively in writing and orally, and representing yourself ethically and appropriately. In your written work, you will need to be thorough and thoughtful, spend a good amount of time editing and re-editing your work, and be ethical in representing your skills and experience. Orally, or in person, you will need to be efficient with your choice of words, and you must dress and act appropriately for the role of teacher. Express confidence without exuding it, and make those around you feel comfortable and at ease. At each stage of the employment-seeking process, you will need to be a professional and treat yourself and others around with dignity and respect.

Self-representation can take many forms, including those beyond emails, letters, and phone or in-person contact with future employers. With technology playing an increasingly important role of self-expression and socialization, it is important to ensure that you are representing yourself professionally in all possible forms of communication. This includes the way you present yourself in online communities such as Facebook or MySpace or in personal Blogs and websites. It is becoming increasingly common for employers to search public online "spaces" for additional information about potential future employees. Please make sure that your online materials are appropriate to be viewed by future employers. For additional information about this, see Chapter 7.

Discussion

1. Review your personal social networking sites, blogs, and websites to determine how they may be viewed by future school district hiring committees. Please discuss any concerns you may have about your postings.
2. What kinds of images, discussion topics, or other posted information might school districts be concerned about?
3. Complete an internet search on the theme of teachers and social networking. Discover the current status of employers' impressions of teacher profiles and discuss your findings.

Résumés

You will need to submit a résumé for each position you are applying to. Your résumé is the primary means through which you describe your skills and experiences to potential employers. A résumé is a brief statement that will allow potential employers to compare your skills set and experience to potential job necessities and requisites. The résumé should be confined to one page if possible and it should share, at a glance, what future employers need to know. Many employers prefer an easy-to-read bullet point listing of your most relevant experiences. As building a résumé is very important, not only for your current search but also for all searches in your career, it is advisable to seek additional assistance through your on-campus career services center. Worksheet 6.1 will assist you in gathering your thoughts and materials prior to drafting your résumé and your visit to career services.

Worksheet 6.1
Components of a Résumé

List the following information in order to begin drafting your résumé.

Name and contact information:

- Full name
- Temporary mailing address
- Permanent mailing address
- Phone and fax numbers
- Email address (this should be a professional email address)

Statement of desired position:

- A short description of the position you are seeking. This description may change to fit the different positions you are applying for, or it may be general enough to remain for all possible positions.

Education:

- College or University Information

  - Name and location of college/university
  - Degree title and year awarded
  - Majors and minors
  - GPA
  - Certification
  - If you attended multiple colleges/universities, you must have a separate section listing each attended

Experience:

- In this section, you should only list experiences that have contributed most significantly to your preparation as a music educator.

  - Student teaching
    - Name and location of school
    - Name of cooperating teacher
    - Dates of experience
    - Grade levels and subjects taught
    - Description of additional tasks performed
    - If your student teaching was in more than one location, complete this process with each student teaching location

- ○ Any other teaching including private lessons, camp councilor, work with children or youth, coaching, volunteering assistance with youth ensembles, any significant musical performances that were an ongoing paid position, etc.

Honors and awards:

- Scholarships or grants received
- Recognition of academic excellence such as honor rolls
- Recognition of musical excellence

Membership in professional organizations:

Optionally, a listing of musical accomplishments or significant performances:

For examples of résumés, see the following websites and text:

http://www.menc.org/careers/view/a-career-guide-for-music-education-2nd-ed Free samples of resumes for music educators provided by the National Association for Music Education.

http://www.collegegrad.com/resumes/ Information provided for recent college graduates. Free résumé templates are provided as well as information on cover letters and interviews.

Enelow, W. S., & Kursmark, L.M. (2001). *Expert Resumes for Teachers and Educators.* Indianapolis, IN: Jist Works.

Professional Portfolio

Many student college and university music education programs highly suggest that students create a professional portfolio to assist in the job search and interview process. The portfolio may be a paper version, maintained in a well-organized binder, or an electronic document, such as a website, compact disk or flash drive. Your college or university may have very specific guidelines as to what should be included in a portfolio in terms of evidence or artifacts or they might suggest items that potential employers may be interested in seeing.

Artifacts to Include in a Teaching Portfolio

Possible materials that future employers may want to see in a professional portfolio:

- General information about you, including your likes and interests and what makes you unique
- Professional résumé
- Your philosophy or vision of teaching
- Teaching examples

  ○ Unit/lesson plans for various grade levels or teaching environments
  ○ Samples of student work
  ○ Assessment plans
  ○ Technology samples and your reflections on teaching

- Classroom management plan
- Professional development plan.

If your portfolio is electronic, you may wish to include some of the following:

- Videos and/or audio recordings

- ○ Samples of your conducting
- ○ Samples of your performing as a musician
- ○ Sample of your teaching or working with children/youth (if you have permissions to record students)

There are several activities and worksheets that have been completed throughout this text that may find a welcome place within your professional portfolio.

FIGURE 6.2. Courtesy of Eastern Washington University 2009.

Finding Employment Opportunities

Prior to the completion of student teaching, you will likely begin looking for your first teaching job. There are numerous avenues for seeking employment, including both informal and formal means. Informally, you may hear about open positions from cooperating teachers, peers, or university faculty. Formally, you may spend a good amount of time seeking out positions online or in person from various organizations such as your state music education association, career services, or individual school district or state websites.

Most colleges and universities have a career services or placement office to assist in finding employment. Many professional organizations, such as your state music education organization, often list job opportunities on their websites, and sometimes allow school districts to conduct interviews at their state conference. Larger school districts often hold job fairs, and sometimes several school districts will combine efforts in a regional job fair. Many positions can be found online through detailed job searches. The key to finding positions in your desired area is to become familiar with which sites are most applicable to your search. In order to do this, you should ask your university supervisor or career services office for assistance.

Discussion

1. What assistance does the college or university career services office provide during a job search?

    a. What materials must you provide this office to get assistance?

    b. What experience does this office have in seeking education positions?

2. What job-seeking opportunities are provided by local music organizations?

3. Are there online job search engines at the state or school district level?

    a. What is the best way to navigate online searches?

In addition to seeking out posted or advertised positions, you may chose to apply for jobs in a particular desired location or area that do not currently have music positions posted. Some school districts will allow you to submit an application where there is no posted position, while others may not. You are encouraged to contact specific school district human resources personnel to ask questions when needed.

Once you have begun the job search process, it is important that you maintain information about open positions. Each job opening will require different materials to be submitted, including a cover letter, résumé, application, and references. Use worksheet 6.2 to assist you in keeping your job search organized.

Worksheet 6.2
Organizing the Job Search

Create a list of the resources and websites you have found most helpful in your job search:

Use the following table to organize your job search. As you identify a position of interest, add it to the table below and track your progress in the application process over time.

School Name	District Name	Location of Advertisement	Job Description	Due Date	Status			Materials Required				
					Not Started	In Progress	Completed	Cover Letter	Résumé	Application	References	Other

Selecting References

Selecting your references is a very important part of the employment process. The key to selecting references is to choose people who can best and most positively speak about your potential as a music educator. It is common to ask your cooperating teachers to serve as a reference. In fact, if they are not included in your references, it leaves room for speculation as to whether or not they were willing to serve in that role. Another common reference is the university supervisor. They have many years of experience in serving in this role and have observed your teaching as an outsider to the student teaching classroom, and may have known you prior to student teaching as a university student. It may also be common to ask other professionals who have known you as an educator or musician. College or university ensemble directors may be a good choice, as well as any education faculty with whom you have worked.

Once you have selected those whom you would like to ask, it is a good idea to talk through these choices with a cooperating teacher or your university supervisor, both of whom have experience in assisting music educators in the job process. Once the list has been secured, you must formally ask each reference if they would be willing to serve in this capacity. While there may be references you have used in the past for other positions associated with different career fields, it is important that each reference you select at this point is specific to music and music education.

At this stage, it is a good idea to ask your university career services, or whichever on-campus office that maintains your placement file, if confidentially is an important issue in your state. It may be helpful to inform your references upfront if their letters of recommendation would be confidential or available for you to view. You cannot assume that each person you ask is willing to or able to serve as a referee. If a person you have asked to serve as a referee is unable to do so, try to find another person who knows you in a similar way to serve in that role.

Applications and Supporting Materials

Once you have found positions of interest, completed your résumé, and identified references, you will need to begin combining materials for the application process. Most positions have a detailed and specific application. This process, either paper or electronic, typically consists of the submission of a cover letter, your résumé, the completion of an application, and letters of recommendation or completion of standardized recommendation forms.

A cover letter, like any professional letter, must be perfected to represent your abilities in the highest regard. This one-page letter introduces you to school administrators and should be specific to the job for which you are applying. The purpose of the letter is to spark the reader's interest in learning more about you and, therefore, reading your résumé. Your cover letter should be enthusiastic and should showcase your skills and experience in a concise manner. Cover letters should be addressed to a specific person, by name if possible, and should reference the specific job description and your personal ability to fulfill the duties. While you may have some key phrases that can remain the same on various cover letters, do not expect to use the same cover letter for every position to which you are applying. Most administrators use the cover letter to determine the extent to which you have read the job description and the extent to which you may be qualified for that specific position.

Applications vary tremendously from one school district to another and may be either paper or electronic. Some districts' applications may be relatively straightforward, often asking for repetition of materials you have included in your résumé. Do note that if an application asks for redundant information from your résumé, you must include the information, as requested, on the application. Many districts will use the application as the main source of information during the hiring process. Other districts may have more complicated forms, some of which may require long answers, essays, or samples of your writing on a specific theme. The key to answering these longer questions is to ensure you understand exactly what the question is asking. Do not use the same long answers or essay responses on different applications without making sure they answer the specific question precisely. Before you submit an application, it is important to ensure you have completed all questions. It is a good idea to have a friend review the application before submitting it. On rare occasions, you may be asked to complete an online task such as a personality inventory. There is no way to prepare for this kind of task, so be as honest as possible. You may also be asked to submit official college or university transcripts. The career center or registrar will be able to assist you in ordering these materials.

It is common for school districts to request letters of recommendation as part of the application process. Some districts may ask that these letters be sent directly from the recommender, some may request that your placement file be sent from your university, and others may ask that they be sent along with your materials by you directly. Many districts are now requesting that recommenders complete a specific district recommendation form that asks them to judge or comment on your abilities as compared to the aims and objectives of the district. Regardless of the form of recommendation, it is very important that you communicate with the person writing your reference and be sure that you give them as much time as possible to complete their recommendation. In terms of recommendations that must be sent directly by the recommender to the district, you must provide any needed forms and a pre-addressed, postage paid envelope. Remember that your referees are going out of their way to assist you and you need to make the process as easy as possible for them. Each time you use someone's name as a reference for a job application, you should inform them, so they are aware they may be contacted.

Some school districts may require proof of teacher certification as part of the application process. If you have your certificate, be sure that you submit a photocopy of the document and not an original. If you have recently graduated and have yet to receive your official certificate, speak to your university supervisor or on-campus certification office, as there may be assistance available to you, such as university letters which state the status of your certificate.

Interviews

The interview process may be viewed as a nerve-raking experience for some people. The key to successful interviewing is being prepared. Preparation includes simple elements such as locating the interview site, deciding what to wear, and practicing how to present yourself professionally, as well as more complex tasks such as preparing for potential interview questions and designing and practicing sample lessons.

Scenario 6.1

Lisa was invited to interview for an elementary music position in a school located approximately 40 miles from her university campus. Estimating that the drive during rush hour would take her approximately an hour, she left campus an hour and a half prior to the interview. When she arrived at the elementary building she parked, entered the building, introduced herself to the office staff and excitedly stated that she was there to interview for the open music position. A bit startled, the staff members told her that the interview was taking place at the district office, approximately five miles from the school.

Lisa raced to her car, drove to the district building, found parking, and ran into the building. When she arrived, she was directed to a conference room for the interview. When she opened the door, she discovered that it was a group interview and that several other candidates were already present and the interview was apparently underway. A bit flustered, Lisa briefly explained the confusion, apologized, and did her best to slide into interview mode. By the end of the interview, Lisa was calm and comfortable. She felt that she had done a wonderful job answering the interview questions and that she was most likely the best candidate for the position.

Discussion

1. What could Lisa have done to better prepare for this interview experience?
2. What would your first impression of Lisa have been?
3. How does Lisa's behavior in showing up late for the interview, even with a possibly understandable reason, influence your perception of her as a candidate?
4. What do you feel are the most important qualities administrators are looking for in an initial interview?

While you may feel elated when asked to come for an interview, it's important that you maintain professionalism and continue to prepare for success. When you are invited to interview for a position, you need to prepare yourself to ensure you are aware of all the needed information to arrive on time, at the correct location, with a clear vision of how the interview process will be conducted, and that you carefully choose which additional materials to bring along. Some questions you may wish to ask are included below:

- What is the location of the interview?
- Where should I park?
- Are there any protocols for entering the school or district building?
- Is there a specific format for the interviews? Will I be the only person interviewing for the position at that time?
- Should I be prepared to demonstrate my teaching?
- Are there any additional materials you suggest I should bring with me?

There are multiple styles of interviewing. The most common is an individual interview in front of a panel. The panel typically consists of a school administrator, such as a principal or vice principal, other teachers from within the school building, and a school district representative, such as a human resources member or a district music supervisor. Additionally, you may have parents and other music faculty on the panel. Some interviews are not individual and may be a larger group interview, where several applicants are interviewing together at the same time. Yet other interviews may ask that you provide a short "live sample" of your teaching in front of the interviewing panel or real students. Your university supervisor will be able to guide you in preparation for either style of interview and will be able to offer advice as to which is more typical in your area. If you are interviewing from a great distance, perhaps out of state, you may be invited for a phone interview. A phone interview is often similar to an in-person interview, but you are advised to speak with your university supervisor for additional information about this kind of interview.

You will always have materials to bring with you for an in-person interview. Of foremost importance, you should bring additional copies of your résumé for distribution. As interviewers are typically meeting many candidates in a single day, it is important that you provide materials to remind them of your skills and experiences when you arrive. You may also wish to bring a hardcopy of your teaching portfolio or examples that represent your experiences from student teaching. Be sure that you offer these materials for their viewing, but do not lead them through the materials or force materials viewing upon them.

There are multiple lists of possible questions that may be used during a music education interview. Many of these are available from various sources online. The National Association for Music Education (MENC) website offers one such list. This list can be found at http://www.menc.org/careers/view/a-career-guide-for-music-education-2nd-ed-interviews.

Seeking Employment   **113**
Discussion

Using the list of questions provided on the National Association for Music Education (MENC) website or using questions you have created, stage mock interviews with your student teaching seminar peers. Ask each seminar member five to ten questions from this list and, upon completion, give each peer meaningful and thoughtful feedback from the perspectives of various kinds of interviewers. Discuss the results as a class.

- What are some possible strategies for ensuring you have time to think about your answers before saying them aloud?
- Are there right and wrong answers in an interview?
- Is it possible to be professional yet still personable?
- How important is honesty when interviewing?
- Being a recent graduate of the certification program you may feel a little insecure with your lack of experience. What is an appropriate way to handle this?

You will also want to bring your own list of questions for your interviewers. You must remember that while they are interviewing you for the position, you are, in a way, interviewing them to determine if this position is a good fit for you. While you may not want to limit your choices too much during an initial job search, you also don't want to end up in a school or community that will make you unhappy. You must remember that you may very well be teaching in this environment for years, and you need to consider your overall satisfaction of living and working in this community. Your questions may be related to teaching load expectations, program funding, the school or district's vision for the music education program, required curriculum or performance schedules, mentorship programs for new teachers, and so forth. Any question that you have is fair game, with the exception of salary. Salary is typically discussed, and sometimes bargained for, after you have been formally offered the position.

Once you have completed an interview, you will experience possibly the hardest part of the process—waiting to hear if you will be offered the position. Most often at the conclusion of the interview, the interview panel or committee will give you some estimate as to when they will make their decision. During this time, there is little you can do beside stay positive and continue your job search by investigating other positions of interest. You should not contact the school building or human resources administration for any reason, other than to notify them if you have taken a different position elsewhere. It is unusual for the district to contact you unless they are offering you the position, so if you have not heard anything within a reasonable amount, for example two to three weeks, it is all right to contact the human resources department to ask if the position has been filled. Do not contact the building principal or secretary.

If you are offered a position, it is highly advisable that you communicate with your university supervisor to guide you through any possible negotiation process. Typically there is a relatively short amount of time in which you will need to either accept or decline the position, but it is ok to take a little while to determine if this is the best fit for you. Be sure to ask the administrator when they will need to know your final decision.

seven
Ethics, Professionalism, and Legal Issues

FIGURE 7.1. Courtesy of Gregory James Walsh.

Throughout your student teaching experience, you will encounter various situations that will require you to ponder issues of ethics and legal responsibilities. These situations may be the result of an encounter with students, parents, school administrators, or school policies, or they may develop as you reach a higher level of reflection in your teaching.

Ethics can be described as a set of moral principles or values that define good and bad in a given situation. As a teacher you are in a role of authority and your ethics will influence the behaviors, teaching and learning patterns, and everyday practices in your classroom. The entire schooling process is based upon the ethical norms that society at large has created and these norms may or may not always be in alignment with your personal belief systems. An experienced teacher has the ability to understand their personal ethics and the ways in which these beliefs affect their teaching and they are able to understand the societal and school ethics that govern how we interact with students, the curriculum, and school policies.

Local, state, and federal laws define many school ethics. These laws include the treatment of students in so far as services available, as well as the basic right of every student to a fair and socially just education. Individual school districts may also have developed policies to further define these moral principles. These laws and principles are in place to ensure that every student is entitled to courtesy and consideration regardless of their physical appearance, ethnic or cultural origin, religion, socioeconomic status, or learning needs.

Personal Ethics

Everyone has a set of values that they hold to be true. These values are the principles by which we set the standards for our behavior. Your personal ethics are the foundation from which you make all decisions including what you plan, teach, create, do and the ways in which you communicate with others. Sometimes this connection to your ethics is on a conscious level, but it is important for you to realize that this connection may also affect you in unintended ways or on a subconscious level. It is important to keep in mind that just as you have a set of beliefs to guide your actions, so do each of your students, their families, your colleagues, and the school building at large.

It is common for ethics and belief systems to be uniquely tied to your generation. What you feel may be appropriate in terms of behavior, communication with others, and professional representation including dress, mannerisms, and speech may not be universal. If you are a younger teacher, you may need to evaluate your ethics in order to understand what you feel is appropriate and then explore the differences you may have with others such as parents, administrators, and colleagues at your school building. Some young teachers have a difficult time "fitting in" and these generational and ethical differences are often a root cause for their difficulties. By understanding your ethics and beliefs, you may more easily navigate through or avoid foreseeable difficulties in the future.

Scenario 7.1

Megan is almost finished with her student teaching in a high school band program. She feels she has grown professionally during the semester and is extremely proud of the wonderful interpersonal connections she has made with her students.

As the students prepare for her departure, they are eager to find ways in which to keep in contact with her. One of her students decides to look on the internet for websites related to Megan as a means for keeping in contact. Megan's personal website is found and, unfortunately, it is more social than professional. It contains multiple pictures of her in flirtatious social attire and partying with her college friends along with a blog in which she and her friends make comments regarding social situations that are not appropriate for high school student viewing. Shocked and excited by what was found, the student decides to forward Megan's website to the rest of the band members.

The following day, Megan is surprised when she is welcomed to class by giggles, pointing, and staring from the majority of students. Finally, a student asks her a suggestive question about her personal life. When asked how the student knows about this issue, Megan is told that the students have viewed her website. She instantly feels fearful and is worried about how this will affect the students' view of her as their teacher. Additionally, she wonders if any parents have seen the website and is concerned that this may become an issue with her cooperating teacher and school administration.

Discussion

1. How could Megan have avoided this situation?
2. How can teachers maintain a separate social and professional life?
3. How are you represented in both real and virtual worlds? Are these sources of information appropriate for student viewing?

Ethical Decision-Making

Most of us like to think of ourselves as just and ethical people, however, the complexity of teaching will often result in challenges that test our ability to be fair and just. As a teacher, you will face difficult and complex situations, and it is not always easy to weigh the issues of wrong and right. Sometimes circumstances may occur that will create a conflict of your values and principles, placing you in a situation of ethical compromise. The following scenario presents a situation in which a student teacher's ethics are challenged.

Scenario 7.2

Bart has just completed his final general music class of the morning and is leaving his classroom to visit the faculty room for a much-needed break. On his way to the faculty room, he becomes aware of a commotion outside a nearby classroom. As he approaches, he witnesses a teacher yelling at a student in the hallway. The student is crying and cowering, but the teacher continues to yell at him regarding his poor behavior in class. Bart views this behavior as very intimidating to the student and wonders if he should do anything about it. Part of him believes that regardless of what the student has done, the behavior by his colleague is inappropriate and should be stopped. Another part of him realizes that he did not witness the student's behavior and feels he should not intervene in another teacher's choice of discipline.

Discussion

1. What would you do in this situation?
2. What are the possible repercussions for choosing to try to stop this behavior?
3. What are the possible repercussions of choosing to do nothing?

Professional Responsibilities

As a student teacher, and eventually a teacher, you will have ethical responsibilities in the teaching profession. These responsibilities include the relationships with colleagues in the school and to students and their families.

Responsibilities Within the School Building

Within the school building, ethics often display themselves most strongly through the notion of professionalism. Throughout your academic preparation, professionalism has been stressed through simple terms such as attendance and punctuality, the manner and timeliness of assignments, and the ways in which you interact with colleagues and professors. All of this training has been to prepare you to be professional in the working world.

As a teacher, you are expected to adhere to school policy and guidelines. In nearly every school distinct or educational setting, there are formal publications stating what is expected of you in terms of professionalism. These often come in the form of

District/Area or School Building manuals and contracts. Additionally, there are multiple laws and regulations that you must be aware of.

Additionally, there are also sets of unspoken guidelines or policies within each school and district that determine what may and may not be deemed appropriate. These guidelines are often not written out, and they commonly consist of elements that must be observed through experience or discussed with colleagues or administrators. These expectations may include appropriate dress, attendance at meetings, extra service commitments through committee work, and how and when to volunteer to assist on larger school wide projects.

An excellent source of help for determining these unwritten guidelines will be in your relationships with in-building colleagues. During your student teaching experience, your cooperating teacher will be the primary source for collegiality, but once you complete student teaching and are working at your own school, you must create professional relationships with colleagues. It is much easier to foster these relationships when you consider the very nature of professionalism, such as completing and submitting your materials, reports, and communications in a timely manner, maintaining a delicate balance between social activities and school relationships, volunteering to work on committees or other large-scale projects, behaving appropriately within the school building or when around your work colleagues, and communicating professionally with others.

It is human nature to partly judge one's professionalism by the ways in which people present themselves physically and socially. A common difficulty for new teachers is finding ways in which to fit in with their new colleagues, especially when there may be significant age differences. One way to combat this difficulty is to make sure that you are dressed appropriately for the role of teacher, are well groomed, use age-appropriate language (and if in doubt, err to the side of being overly professional), and that you portray to others that you are taking your career as a teacher seriously.

As described in scenario 7.1, it is becoming increasingly easier to find information about others online. The boundary between professional and social lives is only as complete as you construct it. It is important that you take into consideration what and how much you want others to know about you in the work place, both socially and professionally. You purposefully create a boundary that both you and your colleagues and students will be comfortable with. Be mindful of all the ways in which you present yourself both inside and outside the school environment. It's a careful balance to maintain your social and professional lives, but with forethought in planning you will be able to do so.

Copyright Laws

Copyright, a form of intellectual property law, protects original works of authorship including literary, dramatic, musical, and artistic works, such as poetry, novels, movies, songs, computer software, and architecture. Copyright does not protect facts, ideas, systems, or methods of operation, although it may protect the way these things are expressed. Under the US Copyright Law, copyright owners have the exclusive right to print, publish, copy, and sell their protected works. The copyright owners of the books and music you purchase usually are indicated on those publications. The intention of the Copyright Law is to encourage the creative works of artists and scientists by ensuring that financial proceeds from materials will go to those who have created them, allowing for further materials to be produced.

In the music classroom, most issues relating to copyright revolve around illegally printing musical scores and materials. It is essential to the future of printed music that the Copyright Law be upheld by all. Composers, arrangers, publishers, and dealers are losing a significant percentage of their income because of illegal photocopying. This loss of revenue ultimately means that less printed music will be available for sale, short print runs of music will increase the cost of printed materials, and dealers will no longer be able to afford to carry large stocks of sheet music.

The following are expressly prohibited under the Copyright Law:

- Copying to avoid purchase
- Copying music for any kind of performance*
- Copying without including copyright notice
- Copying to create anthologies or compilations
- Reproducing material designed to be consumable such as workbooks, standardized tests and answer sheets
- Charging students beyond the actual cost involved in making copies as permitted.

An important element of the Copyright Act that music educators must be aware of is the concept of "Fair Use." Fair Use allows for the extended use of some copyrighted materials in educational settings. Fair Use can be difficult to decipher and the rules are not completely clear. If you are unsure as to how a musical score of materials may be used in the classroom under Fair Use, you must contact the person, publisher, or company owning the copyright.

The three main components of Fair Use that most often affect music teachers are Reproducing, Recording, and Derivative Works. Reproducing a musical score for educational purposes is acceptable as long as the portion reproduced represents 10 percent or less of the full score and does not consist of a single performable unit. In terms of recording, Fair Use allows for a single recording of a performed work to be recorded for educational purposes. It does not allow for copies of this recording to be made or distributed. If additional recordings are desired, you must contact the publisher of each recorded selection and pay a fee based on the total number of recordings you wish to make. If you wish to alter the music score, which is entitled Derivative Works under the

---

* Emergency copying to replace purchased copies which for any reason are not available for an imminent performance is allowable, provided purchased replacement copies shall be substituted in due course.

Fair Use clause, you may do so as long as it does not change the character of the work or alter or add lyrics. More information about Fair Use of copyright in educational settings can be found by visiting the US Copyright Office or Music Publishers association websites.

Scenario 7.3

C.J. was assisting his cooperating teacher after school with preparations for that evening's concert. One of the tasks he had been asked to perform was to check individual student's music folders, to ensure they had all the selections in the correct order for the performance. As C.J. reviewed the folders, he noticed that Kamini, who plays first trombone, was missing a score for one of the selections. C.J checked the music library in an attempt to find an additional score for her to use. Unfortunately, there were no remaining copies. With the concert a few hours away, C.J. made the decision to photocopy the score from another student's folder and place it in Kamini's folder.

Discussion

1. In this situation, was photocopying the score legal?
2. What other options might C.J. have had?

Scenario 7.4

Yi-Ting, was excited to be two weeks away from graduation and successfully completing her student teaching in an elementary general music program. She had had many wonderful experiences in this classroom and felt very supported and liked by her cooperating teacher. She enjoyed this experience so much, she was hoping to find an elementary general music teaching position upon graduation.

After teaching several third-grade music classes, Yi-Ting's cooperating teacher asked her to take some materials down to the office for photocopying. When she arrived at the office and began to look at the materials, she found that she was being asked to photocopy 35 copies of a full octavo for the elementary choir. As she began to lay the first page on the glass, she noticed a flyer of the US Copyright regulations posted over the photocopy machine. She felt very guilty and decided not to make the copies. All the way back to the classroom she was concerned about her decision and what repercussions, if any, there would be from her cooperating teacher. This was an especially difficult decision, with her final evaluation and letter of recommendation from her cooperating teacher coming soon.

Responsibilities to Students

Every student is entitled to your respect, courtesy, and considerate actions regardless of their ethnicity, socioeconomic status, physical appearance, aptitude, or religious or cultural preferences. You may find that you build rapport with certain students over others, but you cannot let this impede upon your fair treatment of all students. You may never intimidate, humiliate, or demoralize a student, nor judge them unfairly for their differences. Your students have the right to express their feelings, thoughts, and ideas as openly as you express your own. You may not impose your political or religious views on students and you must maintain a balance of both sides on any controversial topic.

As a teacher, you have the responsibility to look to the welfare of your students in all situations. This responsibility includes how you maintain order and handle disciplinary actions, ensure students' personal safety both inside and outside the classroom, and maintain up-to-date knowledge of laws and policy regarding students' rights.

Disciplinary Actions

The discipline of students is inevitable in most teaching situations. There are many legal issues regarding the forms of discipline that may be used and you must become aware of both law and local policy before initiating any form of discipline. A major key to being successful in your use of discipline is to ensure that students are aware of your expectations for their behavior prior to any kind of altercation and to have a sequence of disciplinary actions, or consequences, in place. These actions should be based upon school building and district policy and must be communicated with students at the start of the school year. It is of utmost importance that you maintain a record of all disciplinary actions that you are involved in. This will help you to understand which approaches work best for each student, know the amount of disciplinary action each student has received, and will serve as a permanent record should your actions be called into question by the student, their parents, or the school administration. It has become increasingly common for teachers to be questioned about the action they take in regards to discipline and you must be purposeful in the ways in which you maintain evidence of your responses.

Discipline within the classroom primarily takes place through verbal control, which can be defined as the use of oral and body language by the teacher. While this form of discipline is typically acceptable, it is important to know that it may be liable should it result in emotional damage to the student. As evident in scenario 7.2, it may be difficult to determine the threshold of appropriateness with this form of discipline. To make sure you do not cross the line, you must always maintain emotional control and avoid reference to the student's character or personality, keeping the focus on the student's behavior. The end result of any disciplinary action should be for the benefit of the individual student and the classroom operations as whole and not as a means of humiliation or extreme authoritative control.

There may be incidents around you that require physical intervention. You must become familiar with your individual school policy on this matter. According to Federal Law, corporal punishment does not violate the Eighth Amendment, which bars cruel and unusual punishment, but it is illegal in more than half the states and in multiple local school districts. In all cases, it is best not to discipline a student in any physical way through touching or striking or through the expectation that they will complete some form of physical task for their misbehavior. Under no circumstances should a student be touched in a harmful manner unless there is an imminent physical threat to you or another student. Typically, physical intervention takes place in the protection of yourself against a student who is threatening bodily harm, protecting one student from physically injuring another, or stopping a student from destroying school property. As a student teacher, it is best to seek the assistance from your cooperating teacher in all matters that may require physical intervention. Being a student teacher, and essentially a guest in the school building, you may not have the same legal protections an employed teacher in that school building possesses.

If a student is suspected of having illegal possessions, such as weapons, drugs, or obscene materials, within the school building or on school grounds, there may be a need for their personal belongings to be searched. Search and seizure is typically legal within the school system due to the need to maintain a safe environment for all students. If you suspect a student is carrying illegal materials and you have evidence that may warrant an investigation, you are *strongly* advised to contact your administrators. As a student teacher, or even as a classroom teacher, *do not* search a student's body or clothing for harmful items. According to your school building's policy, it may be necessary to contact local law authority to complete any search and seizure on school grounds.

You may have a student who is injured within your classroom or must take routine medication during the school day. The general policy is to send the student to the appropriate medical officer within the school building, typically the school nurse. If it is a true medical emergency, contact administration immediately, make the child as comfortable as possible, and ask for the assistance from fellow teachers until help is available. Do not treat an injury unless it is absolutely necessary.

Confidentiality and Child Abuse

It is common for students to befriend teachers, particularly in the music classroom where the relationships between teachers and students are slightly more personal. It is not uncommon for students to discuss parts of their personal lives with you. If students confide in you, they typically expect that their secrets will not be shared with others. This is easy to comply with unless you feel the student is in some form of physical or emotional danger. Most states consider teachers to be Mandated Reporters, meaning that if you suspect the child or youth is being abused, whether they have verbalized this or not, you must take your concerns to administrators and the authorities. The common forms of abuse are: physical abuse, neglect, sexual abuse, and emotional abuse.

Possible Warning Signs of Abuse

Physical abuse: cuts or lacerations, missing teeth, fractures, rope or cigarette burns, excessive bruising in unusual places, fear of leaving school or returning home, constant unexplained injuries

Neglect: incessant fatigue, excessive hunger, uncleanliness, body odor, wearing the same clothing for multiple days in a row

Sexual abuse: difficulty walking or sitting, torn or stained underclothes, shame or self-loathing

Emotional abuse: low self-esteem, behavioral extremes, frequent outbursts, demands for affection, social isolation, fear of physical closeness or extreme desire for physical closeness, inability to communicate needs appropriately with others

---

Disability Legislation

As a music teacher, it is important to understand the rights of students with disabilities. You have most likely taken previous coursework on this topic and now, during your student teaching, you will be called to put that knowledge into action. In short, all students have the right to free public education in the least constrictive environment. This means that disabled students have the right to be educated with their peers in public schools with any special services that may be needed provided, with no fees or added costs to their families. Once a child with special needs has been identified and evaluated and it has been determined what special assistance would best fit their needs, he or she will be placed in a regular classroom setting if appropriate. All students, regardless of ability, should have equal access to all school activities, including music and the arts. Some children may be mainstreamed into the music classroom, while others may require a more individualized approach, such as music lessons taught in a self-contained setting.

Discussion

- How much do you know about disability legislation?
- At this point in your student teaching, what kinds of experiences have you had in working with disabled or special needs students? Please discuss.
- How have you or your cooperating teacher adapted or altered the curriculum, class materials, or particular assignments to assist students with disabilities or special needs?
- Do you feel the music classroom(s) you are working in currently is/are conducive to disabled or special needs students?
- Have you been involved with the creation or implementation of an Individual Educational Plan (IEP) for a disabled or special needs student? How much do you know about this process?

Explore the following disability legislation using texts from previous coursework, library materials, or the internet.

- Elementary and Secondary Education Act (1965, P.L. 89–10)
- Vocational Rehabilitation Act, Section 504 (1973 P.L. 93–112)
- All Handicapped Children Act (1975, P.L. 94–142)
- Individuals with Disabilities Education Act (1990, P.L. 101–336)
- The Developmental Disabilities Assistance and Bill of Rights Act Amendments (1994, P.L. 101–336)
- The Individuals with Disabilities Education Improvement Act (1997, P.L. 108–446)
- The Individuals With Disabilities Education Improvement Act (2004, P.L. 108–446)

eight
Continued
Professional
Growth

FIGURE 8.1. Courtesy of Hans Splinter.

The end of student teaching is often the beginning of a music teaching career. While the primary focus of this text has been on the student teaching process, it is important to know that once you have completed this experience you will become fully responsible for your own continued professional growth. This chapter will discuss ways in which you, as a music educator, can remain active in the profession through your relationship with others, membership in organizations, conference attendance, and continued educational opportunities such as additional certifications and graduate-level course work.

Building Local Relationships

After years of being a student and a period of time being a student teacher, it can be difficult to make the transition to becoming the teacher. During your student teaching experience, you have most likely relied upon the guidance of your cooperating teacher(s) and others such as your university supervisor, seminar peers, and university faculty members. As you make the transition to teacher, it will serve you well to begin to foster new relationships within your locale to create a support system.

Many school buildings or school districts offer mentoring programs for new teachers. If you have not been advised about this kind of program in your area, you are encouraged to ask your school administration if this kind of support is available. Sometimes you will be paired with a music teacher in your building or district and other times you may be paired with an experienced teacher in a different discipline. If there is not a formal mentor program available through your school or district, you may wish to seek out an experienced teacher with whom you feel comfortable to serve in this role.

In addition to a school- or district-sponsored mentor, it may be beneficial to create or maintain relationships outside your direct teaching environment. Examples of people you may choose to consider as additional mentors would be university faculty members with whom you have worked, peers with whom you shared the student teaching seminar course, and your previous cooperating teachers. Having support from those outside your immediate teaching environment may offer different or new perspectives on the situations you encounter and they may serve as unbiased listeners.

As a teacher, you are assumed to act as an adult regardless of your age or maturity level. Unlike many other professions where there is a fairly defined line between work and social behavior, in teaching, your behaviors are often observed and scrutinized outside the classroom as well as in. This is particularly true if you live within the service area boundaries in which your school resides. It is a careful balance to maintain your personal and professional lives, and as an educator you must be mindful to maintain the ethical stature of a teacher.

Scenario 8.1

During the past few years, Mr. Armstrong's advanced high school choir has competed at a high caliber regional choir festival. While his choir has performed well in the past, it has yet to receive a perfect score. This has been very frustrating for him and he is beginning to believe that a perfect score will always be out of reach. Mr. Armstrong has made doing well at the festival this year a priority and he has sacrificed other parts of his curriculum and schedule to ensure that the choir has enough time to prepare.

On the night of the choir festival, Mr. Armstrong's choir performed beautifully. He was delighted to hear that finally, after so many years, the choir received a perfect score! Upon returning to school Mr. Armstrong decided to visit a local restaurant with a few of the choir's chaperones to celebrate their performance. When they arrived, one of the parents ordered a beer for Mr. Armstrong, which he gladly accepted. After a few minutes, several of the choir members also entered the restaurant. They came to Mr. Armstrong's table to talk about how well they had sung. They had been standing for a few moments when he finally invited them to sit down at their table.

The next morning, Mr. Armstrong was called into the principal's office. Convinced that he was going to be congratulated on the choir's perfect score, he hustled down to the office before classes began. When he entered the principal's office, he was asked to sit down while the principal informed him that a parent has called to complain that he was seen drinking in front of the choir students the previous evening. Mr. Armstrong was told that this incident was being forwarded to the district level and it is likely Mr. Armstrong will be disciplined for his actions.

Discussion

1. How do you feel about Mr. Armstrong having had a drink in front of his students after returning from the performance?
2. Why might this behavior have upset a parent?
3. Do you feel his actions are worthy of disciplinary action?
4. How could Mr. Armstrong have better separated his professional and personal life in this situation?

If you move to take a position in an unfamiliar location, it is important that you make friends both within the school building and in your home environment. While you may very well create friendships within the school building that cross over to out-of-school relationships, you are encouraged to also create friendships with those outside the school environment. By doing so, you may be able to more easily step away from teaching during the evening and weekend hours. As a musician, participation in local community ensembles may assist you to create new friendships and will keep you performing on your voice or instrument. While you are making the transition to professional music educator, it is important that you maintain your identity as a musician and that you continue to express your love of music-making for your own personal satisfaction.

Building Professional Relationships

There are a number of professional organizations that are available to assist you with your continuing professional growth. Table 8.1 is a listing of some such organizations. There are three main opportunities that organizations provide including networking with other music educators, access to publications and other materials and the attendance at conferences and workshops.

Networking through organizations is an excellent way to find others, both locally and nationally, who share common interests in and ideas about music teaching and learning. Several organizations host online blogs that allow for members to ask questions of one another and share current ideas. Another great attribute of membership in organizations are the publications and materials that become available to you. Journals, newsletters, repertoire and material lists, and, in some cases, materials themselves are available for member use. Many of the organizations listed in Table 8.1 offer journals that contain the most current music education research and practices.

Conferences are the primary means by which educators share and learn from one another. You are highly encouraged to seek out conference opportunities in your area of interest. Typically conference sessions that have been accepted for presentation represent the highest quality of thought and preparation and are given by leading scholars and teachers in their given field. Some school buildings or districts may provide funding to support your attendance at conferences, but regardless of cost it is in your best interest to attend as many as reasonably possible. Some organizations offer festival and performance opportunities for students as well.

Maintaining Certification or Licensure

Once you have received your teaching certification or licensure, it is important to ensure that you understand all of the conditions surrounding its maintenance. In many states, your initial teaching certificate or license is preliminary and you must complete additional coursework or attend workshops in order to reach a minimum number of hours or experience for renewal or to progress to a more comprehensive certificate. For additional information about your certification/licensure, contact your on-campus certification/licensure office or the state department of education.

TABLE 8.1 Music organizations

Organization Title	Description	National/ International	State	Regional
National Association for Music Education (MENC)	MENC is the world's largest arts education organization and the only association that addresses all aspects of music education. More than 142,000 members and supporters represent all levels of teaching from preschool to graduate school. http://www.menc.org/	X	X	X
American Choral Directors Association (ACDA)	ACDA membership consists of choral directors who represent more than one million singers across the United States. ACDA members teach choral music in public and private schools—kindergarten through senior high school—and at college and university levels. They conduct a variety of choral groups, including boys' choirs, children's choirs, men's and women's choruses, junior and senior high school choirs, college and university choruses, ethnic choirs, vocal-jazz ensembles, and symphony choruses. They also conduct choirs in their communities and in their places of worship. http://acda.org/	X	X	X
The National Band Association (NBA)	NBA, founded on September 11, 1960, is the largest band directors' professional organization in the world. It was organized for the purpose of promoting the musical and educational significance of bands and is dedicated to the attainment of a high level of excellence for bands and band music. http://www.nationalbandassociation.org/	X	X	X
American String Teachers Association (ASTA)	ASTA, founded more than 60 years ago, is a membership organization for string and orchestra teachers and players, helping them to develop and refine their careers. ASTA's members range from budding student teachers to artist-status performers. The organization provides a vast array of services, including instrument insurance, an award-winning scholarly journal, discounts	X	X	

TABLE 8.1 (*continued*). Music organizations

	on publications and resources, annual professional development opportunities, and access to collegial network of colleagues throughout the string profession. http://www.astaweb.com			
Organization of American Kodály Educators (OAKE)	The mission of the Organization of American Kodály Educators is to enrich the quality of life of the people of the USA through music education by promoting the philosophy of Zoltán Kodály. https://oake.org/default.aspx	X		X
Dalcroze Society of America (DSA)	DSA is a non-profit educational organization that welcomes musicians, dancers, actors, therapists, and artist-educators who study and promote the Dalcroze Eurhythmics approach to music learning through rhythmic movement, aural training, and improvisation. http://www.dalcrozeusa.org	X	X	X
American Orff– Schulwerk Association (AOSA)	The American Orff–Schulwerk Association is a professional organization of music and movement educators dedicated to the creative teaching approach developed by Carl Orff and Gunild Keetman. Joined by the belief that learning about music—learning to sing and play, to hear and understand, to move and create—should be an active and joyful experience. http://www.aosa.org	X	X	
International Society for Music Education (ISME)	ISME was formed at a conference convened by UNESCO in 1953 "to stimulate music education as an integral part of general education." This has been ISME's main concern over the past decades and continues to be its most important source of motivation. In the years that followed its formation, ISME gradually evolved to what it is today: a worldwide service platform for music educators who want their profession to be taken seriously by educators in other disciplines, by politicians and policy makers, by international organizations that promote culture, education, conservation and durable development of cultural heritage. http://www.isme.org	X		X

It is common to meet requirements for renewal by taking graduate level course work that is pertinent to your teaching area or by attending workshops that have been accredited by the state in which you are teaching. Several kinds of in-service courses or workshops will offer certification in a particular methodology or approach in addition to offering university credit or participation hours. Taking courses, attending workshops, or gaining additional certification in a particular methodology are excellent opportunities to hone your teaching skills, learn new approaches for use in your classroom, gain expertise in a particular area, and increase your marketability and standing within the profession.

Discussion
In your student teaching seminar, share your answers to the following questions:

1. What are the state expectations for continuing your certification of licensure?
2. Will your certification or licensure expire? If so, how long do you have to renew your certification or licensure and what is required for renewal?
3. What methodologies or approaches offer their own specific certification?

In some states, completion of a graduate degree is required during your career as a professional educator. In other states, it is not a requirement but is fairly easily attainable through the compilation of university credits accumulated through certification/licensure requirements. Some music educators elect to complete a graduate degree solely out of personal interest. If you are considering graduate studies, there are several issues you must think about.

Graduate degrees in music typically fall into two main categories: academic degrees and performance degrees. Academic degrees in music are from the fields of music education, musicology, music theory, composition, and ethnomusicology. Performance degrees in music typically consist of conducting or performance in a particular studio such as piano, voice, clarinet, or viola. If you are considering what kind of program to enroll in, you must look carefully at your intended future and what specifically you would like to gain from this degree.

Beginning Your Teaching Career

When you begin your first teaching position, you will not find perfection. You will find the real world as it exists everywhere, with the good along side the bad. It is likely that your first teaching position may be different than you imagined. You may have imagined teaching a certain grade level or having a particular kind of ensemble. Or you may have imagined teaching in a specific geographical location or with a group of students who have particular characteristics. Despite any differences between the imagined and reality, you will most certainly find students in need of a compassionate, caring, motivated, and knowledgeable music teacher to guide their learning and foster their love for music.

There will be beauty, joy, success, improvement, and fun, just as there will be disappointment, struggle, disheartenment, difficulty and occasional failure. This balance may shift on a daily or even hourly basis as you ride the ebb and flow that is teaching, but have faith—you are serving society in an integral way. Teaching is one of the greatest humanistic professions in the world. Whenever you face challenges, just remember that ours is a profession of worth. Celebrate the successes and learn from the difficulties. Strive to accept every student for what they bring to the classroom environment. Work diligently to understand your students' needs and capabilities and find creative ways to push their potential. You have been drawn to teaching for important reasons, those reasons being your love of music and of children and youth. You owe it to them and to yourself to make the most of this calling!